Freire and Environmentalism

FREIRE IN FOCUS

Series editors: Greg William Misiaszek and Carlos Alberto Torres

This series of short-format books provide readers a diverse range of Paulo Freire's work and Freireans' reinventions towards social justice both inside and outside education, without readers needing any prior knowledge of his scholarship. The books which offer new perspectives on the work of Freire's teaching, ideas, methods, and philosophies. Each book will introduce Freire's work so it is easily understood by a wider audience without overly simplifying the depth of his scholarship.

Advisory Board

Freire and Environmentalism
Ecopedagogy

GREG WILLIAM MISIASZEK

BLOOMSBURY ACADEMIC
LONDON • NEW YORK • OXFORD • NEW DELHI • SYDNEY

BLOOMSBURY ACADEMIC
Bloomsbury Publishing Plc
50 Bedford Square, London, WC1B 3DP, UK
1385 Broadway, New York, NY 10018, USA
29 Earlsfort Terrace, Dublin 2, Ireland

BLOOMSBURY, BLOOMSBURY ACADEMIC and the Diana logo are
trademarks of Bloomsbury Publishing Plc

First published in Great Britain 2023

Series design by Charlotte James
Cover image © Paulo Freire via Torres, Carlos Alberto (2014).
First Freire: Early writings in social justice education. Teachers College
Press. Background image © ilyast / Getty Images

A catalogue record for this book is available from the British Library.

A catalog record for this book is available from the Library of Congress.

ISBN: HB: 978-1-3502-9210-9
PB: 978-1-3502-9209-3
ePDF: 978-1-3502-9211-6
eBook: 978-1-3502-9212-3

Series: Freire in Focus

Typeset by Newgen KnowledgeWorks Pvt. Ltd., Chennai, India
Printed and bound in Great Britain

To find out more about our authors and books visit www.bloomsbury.com
and sign up for our newsletters.

CONTENTS

FIGURE

SERIES EDITORS' FOREWORD

Carlos Alberto Torres, Distinguished Professor of Education and Director, Paulo Freire Institute, UCLA.

> I do not believe in loving among women and men, among human beings, if we do not become capable of loving the world. Ecology has gained tremendous importance at the end of this century. It must be present in any educational practice of a radical, critical, and liberating nature.[1]

The work of Paulo Freire is exemplary in linking theory and research, producing frameworks for educating global citizens, including building community and mutual respect; creating social responsibility, instilling an appreciation for diversity, and promoting multiple literacies and conflict-solving approaches within the framework of social justice education. Freire "speaks of the pleasure of breathing pure air, the joy of entering a river that has no pollution, of stepping on grass, or the sand on the beach. He criticized the capitalist logic that gives no value to those free pleasures, and substitutes for them the pleasure of profit … not human needs, but needs imposed upon human beings by the search for profits. Freire did not separate human needs from the needs of the planet. When he died, Freire was writing a book about ecology."[2]

Ecopedagogy is the linchpin of the elective affinity between global citizenship and sustainability in terms of implementation and public policy orientations, particularly in the fields of education. Ecopedagogy is also one of the tools to promote planetarian citizenship—a concept that needs an analytical and normative definition. Without a global ethics based on human rights in democracy, and the link between global citizenship and sustainability to protect the planet, while we seek to live fructiferous lives, the neoliberal model will deepen the crises of democracies, the crises of world's peace and keep undermining the health of our planet.

This book is about Freire as an ecopedagogue. As Freire stressed that education should help students critically reading the world as a tool to overcome oppressions, ecopedagogy grounded in Freire's work teaches literacy to read the world as part of Earth. This is essentially what Misiaszek argues, alongside with other Freireans ecopedagogues, in this book.

Teaching ecopedagogical literacy helps students read the politics of anti-environmental acts, which is crucial for praxis to take action to end the deep-rooted causes for environmental injustices. This is opposite to most environmental teaching that superficially teaches the causes and effects of unsustainable acts, further separating environmental injustices and social injustices. Ecopedagogy is crucial to save us and the planet overall from a total catastrophy of environmental devastation. Hopefully, this book will act as a catalyst to a widened audience for further exploration needed for ecopedagogical teaching and scholarship in our time and age.

Introduction

What are the costs of environmental violence, who suffers from it, and who benefits from it? I have started many of my publications with this question.[1] Without benefits from acts of environmental violence for anyone, the acts would not be consciously done. For example, there is no reason to drill deep into ocean floors for a slippery, viscous fluid (i.e., oil) unless it serves some perceived purpose. Oil does serve numerous purposes, such as fuel, lubrication, and plastic production. However, without needing to be said, numerous factors of oil production, usage, and distribution cause social and environmental oppressions and dominations.

"Costs" are far beyond economic ones, including costs of social injustices, which are inseparable from environmental violence and the costs of the destruction of Nature beyond humans' interests. This key question is critically problem-posed in ecopedagogical spaces for rich, democratic discussions through students' and teachers' diverse perspectives, experiences, and epistemologies (i.e., constructed knowledges and ways of knowing). Ecopedagogy, grounded in the work of Paulo Freire, is teaching students to act in ending oppressions and domination (i.e., praxis) through critical democratic dialogue and reading (i.e., critical literacy) on why environmentally violent acts occur (i.e., ecopedagogical dialogue and literacy). The "whys" primarily emerge from determining the roles of "who benefits" from the violent acts and, in turn, dismisses the suffering of others.

Ecopedagogical goals include "deepening" and "widening" students' and teachers' perspectives of environmental injustices and planetary unsustainability for enacting crucial transformation (Misiaszek, 2018). Deepening indicates teaching to critically understand the impacts of environmental violence locally through the eyes of those who suffer from it. Widening is teaching environmental well-being for all in the world globally *and* the planet holistically. I use the phrase "globally all-inclusive" to emphasize the former, and "planetarily" or "planetarization" emphasizes the latter. This terminology aligns with Neera M. Singh's (2019) calls for widening NIMBY (not-in-my-backyard) to NIAMBY (not-in-anyone's backyard) worldwide and NOPE (not on planet Earth) planetarily wide.

> Environmental Justice struggles are no longer limited to and framed in terms of "Not-in-my-Backyard" (NIMBY) politics, rather EJ [envrionmental justice] activists recognize that a logical extension of NIMBY to NIABY (not-in anyone's backyard) can only be achieved through a loud and clear "NOPE" (Not on Planet Earth)—a clear refusal to activities that generate environmental harms and demand sacrifice zones. (Singh, 2019, p. 138)

Ecopedagogues strive to teach and research for more deepened and widened NIMBY *and* NIAMBY understandings for achieving NOPE goals (Misiaszek, 2020). For example, Singh calls for deconstructing and disrupting "development" by "radical[ly] restructuring of our economies and rethinking our obsession with growth" (Singh, 2019).

"Disrupt" defined: Here and throughout this book, the term "disrupt" signifies an action to counter environmental injustices and unsustainability, including teaching that leads to these outcomes.

"Politics" defined: The critical theories-based concept of the term "politics," used throughout this book, which can be thought of as outside influences upon something, some action, or some happening. It includes, but also is far beyond, the more common association with government and governing policy.

As Freire argued for the need for critical literacy education for reading and rereading the world, ecopedagogical literacy widens reading the world as *part* of the rest of Nature. The "world" is defined as all humans and our interactions, and Nature as all of Earth. This includes reading the inseparability between acts of environmental and social injustices ("socio-environmental" inseparability) and reading Nature beyond that of providing humans' needs and wants (i.e., beyond anthropocentric perspectives). Coinciding with critical, Freirean pedagogies (Gadotti, 1996), ecopedagogy is not just for students to better understand socioenvironmental injustices and unsustainability but teaching the necessary tools for countering both. Students' ecopedagogical praxis emerges from deepened, widened, and diversified self-reflexivity to determine their actions to counter anti-environmentalism.

Ecolinguistical wording: "Earth" is written without the article "the" (i.e., not writing "... the Earth") to not objectify Earth but to write and speak of us (i.e., humans) as *part of* Earth as a living ecological system. This way of communicating coincides with the tenets of ecolinguistics to reconstruct language to value the rest of Nature (Stibbe, 2012, 2014; Derni, 2008; Fill, 2001). In the same reasoning, I capitalize both _N_ature and _E_arth. In addition, the prepositional phrase "the rest of" will always accompany the term "Nature" to signify all that is beyond humans and emphasize that humans are *part of* Nature—that is, the world as *within* Earth.

Determining "who" benefits or suffers from environmental violence is endlessly complex. "Who" can refer to individuals. Or "who" can be populations according to race, gender, ethnicity, sexual orientation, geographic positioning, (non-) spirituality/religiosity, socioeconomic status, citizenship, and numerous other groupings, as well as the intersectionalities between them. The importance of better understanding sociohistorical oppressions placed on specific populations is essential in ecopedagogy. They are termed sociohistorical oppressions to recognize histories of injustice and stress the essentialness of disrupting them, such as ecoracism. "Who" also includes Earth beyond the World, widened to *all* of Nature. The term "planetary sustainability" includes environmentalism outside humans' interests, recognizing that planetary unsustainability is due to our anti-environmental activities.

Differences between justice and domination: Environmental justice only occurs in the world because of justice's reciprocal nature, as Karen Warren (2000) explains through theories of ecofeminism. Humans' ability of reflexivity allows us to be just or unjust; the rest of Nature cannot be (un)just to humans. For example, a natural disaster or a tiger attacking someone is not injustice. In this book, "domination" and "planetary unsustainability" refer to anti-environmentalism beyond the World. These arguments will be further discussed and exemplified throughout this book. "Socio-environmental" will be written both with and without the addition of "planetary sustainability;" however, to somewhat reduce lengthy wording, the use of this phrase will also imply planetary (un)sustainability unless otherwise stated.

This book's beginning paragraphs might seem quite dense with some esoteric terms that are too briefly defined; however, I will further explain and exemplify them throughout the chapters. I will argue the need for ecopedagogy, the essence of Freire within ecopedagogy, how ecopedagogy differs from other environmental pedagogies (e.g., environmental education (EE), education for sustainable development (ESD)), and how ecopedagogical tools should be incorporated within these and other pedagogies. When I use the term "pedagogy(ies)" or "education," it includes how we learn anything, including and beyond schooling (i.e., formal education). For example, environmental learning is how we "know" Nature, see our relationships with the rest of Nature (e.g., Nature as seen as part of or separate from humans), and, in turn, treat Nature. It is important to note that when using the term education, it includes schooling (i.e., formal education), but also informal education (e.g., teaching without formal degrees or certificates given) and informal education (i.e., public pedagogy) which is how we learn anything, such as through movies, social media, and advertisements. Thus, teaching who benefits and who suffers from environmental violence is well beyond traditional classroom walls. When someone learns anti-environmental ideologies from being online, who are the "teachers" is a very complicated and messy question. An example of an ecopedagogical concern for formal education is whether schooling prepares students or not to read and search environmental information on the internet and dismiss information falsely justifying injustices and unsustainability (e.g., post-truths).

Freire's Essence in Ecopedagogy

[Paulo Freire] speaks of the pleasure of breathing pure air, the joy of entering a river that has no pollution, of stepping on grass, or the sand on the beach. He criticized the capitalist logic that gives no value to those free pleasures, and substitutes for them the pleasure of profit ... not human needs, but needs imposed upon human beings by the search for profits. Freire did not separate human needs from the needs of the planet. When he died, Freire was writing a book about ecology. (Gadotti & Torres, 2009, p. 1262)

I will discuss how Freire's work grounds ecopedagogy throughout this book by directly using his own words and from Freireans' contextual reinventions of his work (reinvention will be explained in the last section of this introduction). As the above quote indicates, Freire's next publication before his untimely death was going to focus on ecopedagogy (Gadotti & Torres, 2009; Misiaszek & Torres, 2019). Some of his ecopedagogical work for this publication ended up in his book *Pedagogy of Indignation* (2004). The foundations of Freire's work include, but are not limited to, education through democratic, authentic dialogue; problem-posing approaches that are bottom-up in approach; goals of praxis to end oppressions and domination; historical and political problematizing; transdisciplinary approaches; and saturated with love, utopia, and hope. These are some ecopedagogical foundations that will be unpacked throughout this book.

Ecopedagogues focus on the "whys" of oppressions and domination by determining "who" benefits from unsustainable environmental violence, as well as "how" they benefit. Teaching to understand the "politics" of environmental violence would likely be Freire's way of expressing this focus. Such critical problematizing is opposite to other environmental pedagogies that may or may not have this focus as *part* of teaching.

Unsustainable environmental violence: I write "sustainable" and "unsustainable" continuums of environmental violence because we all utilize Earth's resources for our needs and wants. "Unsustainable environmental violence" emphasizes environmental violence as continuums, from turning on a computer to a transnational corporation polluting rivers globally. We all commit multiple acts of environmental violence every day, but the sustainability of these acts and the possibilities of alternatives is what is essential to teach, learn about, and do. The "unsustainable" aspect is important to teach because environmental violence is not just committed by faceless, "evil" transnational corporations but also us whenever we flip on a light switch or computer, especially when the power is coming from fossil fuels. There are numerous questions to problematize within this example. One is questioning what is "needed" compared to what is "wanted," especially within social justice and sustainability models. Another is asking what are other possible energy sources and what are the politics of oil remaining a primary source of energy.

The title of Freire's most famous book, *Pedagogy of the Oppressed* (2000), indicates how education, including environmental pedagogies, often sustains and/or intensifies sociohistorical oppressions. Posing such questions counters noncritical stances that education is only beneficial—that all "environmental" teaching leads to environmental justice and sustainability. Oppressive pedagogies benefit a select few and negatively affect many others, including the rest of Nature. To effectively sustain hegemony, this truth must be systematically hidden. This veiling coincides with Marx's argument that unjust power can be best gained by instilling notions of false benefits to a population from acts that hurt them the most. Freireans teach to critically unveil false notions of education's neutrality and positivism that hides hegemonic underlying goals.

Instilling education as "neutral," without outside influences, has taught knowledge and ideologies as true without exception (Freire, 2000; Apple, 2004). Thus, students challenging them is abnormal. Positivism, in part, has education or anything in society simplified into a specific, unwavering answer to what is true and/or best. For example, Western sciences are the only legitimate knowledges and ways of knowing about Nature. Both neutrality and positivism were vehemently opposed by Freire (Freire, 1998b).

Another example is "development" taught as based on economic profiteering and all other concerns and aspects of development are devalued. In such teaching, any sense of "sustainable development" is illegitimate when economic profiteering is absent. The politics of neoliberalism in such teaching hides the oppressions and unsustainability from unjust economic profiting that, in turn, strengthens unequal power dynamics. Development taught in this way becomes nontransformable and is better termed as "de-development" for most of the world and "development for unsustainability." Neoliberal _D_evelopment (capitalization of "D" will be explained later) instills economic profiteering without concerns for justice or sustainability to measure everything, including how the rest of Earth is treated.

Freire (2000) argued that falsely portraying education as apolitical is dehumanizing. It is also deplanetarizing and must be actively disrupted by ecopedagogues. False neutrality and positivity are hallmarks of banking education.

> **"(De)planetarizing" defined:** The word "deplanetarizing" signifies the devastation of Nature beyond the world, including outside of the adverse effects on human populations. In other words, deconstructing environmental violence beyond "anthropocentric perspectives (i.e., "non-anthropocentric" lenses) to understand the devastating effects beyond our concerns as humans.

There is no single specific "best" way to teach, with all other ways being "bad." There is no universal step-by-step way of improving education that leads to justice for all with planetary sustainability. I often tell my students that if they read "research" that says if "A," "B," and "C" are done, then "D" will result, no matter the context—run away (metaphorically) from such shallow, positivistic research. This is "technocratic" educational practice and research. One of Freire's most well-known arguments is that education should raise students' critical consciousness (i.e., conscientization, *conscientização* in Portuguese). However, he opposed how many used this argument to utilize step-by-step mechanical approaches. Freire limited his usage of the term in later years (Schugurensky, 2011). There is no specific, universal method or magical mathematical formula that improves education and, in turn, societies everywhere, nor tells us what is truly going on worldwide or planetwide. Thinking of education in this way sustains oppressions by giving supremacy to one way of teaching and conceptualizing all other ways of teaching as inferior. Freire (2000) discussed the dangers of this in various ways, including justifying others', the self, and othered societies as inferior. For example, later in this book, I will discuss how colonizers' positivistic teaching and the West's notion of educational supremacy led to justifying coloniality and currently neocoloniality.

Contested Terrain of (Anti-)Environmental Teaching

> Freire stressed that pedagogies focused on critical discourse are needed to determine the molding ideologies and "clarify the legitimacy of the ethical political dream of overcoming unjust reality … work[ing] against the dominant fatalist ideology and its power to encourage immobility on the part of the oppressed and their adaptation to unjust reality" (Freire, 2004). Freire wrote the following metaphor on controlling ideologies: "Power of ideology makes me think of those dewy mornings when the mist distorts the outline of the cypress trees and they become shadows of something we know is there but cannot really define." (Freire, 1998a, p. 113). (Misiaszek & Torres, 2012, p. 185)

Freire argued that we must constantly deconstruct how education can intensify oppressions to understand how to effectively reconstruct teaching to end oppressions. Ecopedagogical goals can only be achieved by disrupting teaching that justifies environmental violence that dominates Nature and leads to oppressions. This de/reconstruction is not only research on (environmental) pedagogies but within ecopedagogical spaces and curricula.

Prefix usage within (parentheses): My use of prefixes within parentheses before words indicates the possibility of two different aspects of the word or phrase. The term "(environmental)" is in parentheses to indicate the need for de/reconstruction within all learning spaces—spaces labeled as "environmental" and not. Similarly, "(anti-)environmental" emphasizes the point that labeling teaching as "environmental" does not automatically make it so.

For example, my research several years ago in the Appalachia region of the United States, commonly termed as "coal country," unpacked the politics of large, transnational companies "donating" to local schools within lower socioeconomic areas (Misiaszek, 2011). This included "gifting" their "educational materials" on coal and coal mine field trips. Ecopedagogues problematize such questions as: what are the effects of students understanding, or not, the false propaganda of "environmentally good" "clean coal?" How do the companies benefit? And, as Apple (2004) emphasizes, what is the perceived authority that students give to such lessons when the teaching occurs within formal schooling? Apple (2004) argued that the best way to indoctrinate ideologies is to instill them in students as young as possible. These companies in Appalachia are instilling, in part, a commonsense that coal is an essential source of energy without viable alternatives, mining is an integral part of their local cultures and economies, and "clean coal" is "good." All this is gift-wrapped as being "environmental education," indoctrinating ideologies of what is "development," "progress," and increasing "livelihood."

Teaching shallow, superficial understandings of why anti-environmentalism happens will only help to intensify anti-environmentalism. Determining solutions is impossible without knowing the deeper roots of environmental oppressions because their causes and reasons are hidden. Not hidden by mistake, but rather politically and systematically hidden by those benefiting from the oppressions. Their goal is for education to be a tool that leads to the least resistance while committing unsustainable environmental violence. Hidden curricula are constructed by politics within and well beyond classroom walls, schools' campuses, and governmental offices of education (see Giroux, 2001). As in all critical pedagogies, ecopedagogical goals are to teach students how to unveil these roots and then, through dialogue and self-reflexivity, determine necessary actions to disrupt them. Returning to the coal company example, the influences of their falsely generous donations and selection of educational resources illustrate their influences (i.e., politics) in co-constructing curricula without exposing it. Ecopedagogues teach and research to disrupt such teaching/indoctrination.

Freire (2000) gave the following three reasons as to why bottom-up approaches are essential to end oppressions.

- Who is better prepared than the oppressed to understand the terrible significance of an oppressive society?

- Who suffers the effects of oppression more than the oppressed?

- Who can better understand the necessity of liberation? (p. 45)

Bottom-up approaches prioritize understanding and decision-making from those who are oppressed as opposed to top-down meaning-making from dominant entities and "experts," often silencing the voices of the oppressed. Bottom-up understanding of how the coal companies influence curricula begins with hearing from the local populations on how coal leads to environmental violence upon them, their communities, others beyond their communities, and Nature overall. The likelihood of this critical type of learning from coal companies' "gifted" curricula is next to impossible. Here is one of endless examples of politics of education that influence the committing of unsustainable environmental violence.

Ecopedagogical work includes uncovering the hows and the politics of why socioenvironmental connections are not taught or purposely mistaught in education (Misiaszek, 2011, 2018). Throughout this book, I will use the term "ecopedagogical work" to indicate ecopedagogical teaching, literacy/reading, and research, only naming the specific type when directly referenced among the three.

Conscientization of Environmentalism

> Conscientization, seen as a process of criticization of the conscienciousness-world relations, is a condition to assume a human commitment vis-a-vis the historical-social context. In the process of knowledge, human beings tend to commit themselves to reality, as this is a possibility that is related to human praxis. It is through conscientization that subjects assume their historical commitment in the process of making and remaking the world, within concrete possibilities, also making and remaking themselves. (Freitas, 2012, p. 70)

Conscientization of unsustainable environmental violence emerges from critically reading the sociohistorical politics of often-hidden oppressions and domination. Freire stressed the need for reading oppressions through those who are being oppressed to construct possible bottom-up solutions for their liberation (Gadotti, 1996). Teaching students to have this literacy (i.e., ecopedagogical literacy) is ecopedagogues' responsibility.

Freire, in part, utilized Hegel's Master-Slave dialect, which stresses that true power is within the slaves rather than the master(s), to argue that effective solutions can only emerge from below. Why? Because masters are defined by, and obtain/sustain power, from their slaves. Hegel's dialect will be revisited throughout this book. In the first chapter of *Pedagogy of the Oppressed* (2000), Freire initially lays out this argument, which is a foundation of his work overall. Hegel's dialect grounds Freire's disdain for taught ideologies of "success" as the number of people, or metaphoric slaves, "underneath" someone (Freire, 1996, 2000; Gadotti, 1996). If this is "success" or societal goals of "development" by increasing the number of populations under "our" society, neither socio-environmental justice can emerge nor planetary sustainability. This criterion of being "above" others only has the vast majority of the oppressed failing, and the few who become "successful" become oppressors themselves, frequently worse than their prior oppressors (Freire, 2000). Perverted notions of success and development are not transformative but only shift the oppressed-to-oppressor for injustices and domination to continue. Unfortunately, perceptions of controlling the rest of Nature as signs of success are widely held, especially through beliefs of Western exceptionalism and human supremacy.

Conscientization of the masses in recognizing their power to enact transformation is essential, as Freire (2000) points out below.

How can the oppressed as divided, unauthentic beings, participate in developing the pedagogy of their liberation? [Freire's answer:] Only as they discover themselves to be "hosts" of the oppressor can they contribute to the midwifery of their liberating pedagogy ... pedagogy makes oppression and its causes objects of reflection by the oppressed, and from that reflection will come their necessary engagement in the struggle for their liberation. And in the struggle this pedagogy will be made and remade. (Freire, 2000, p. 48)

Ecopedagogical teaching for students to unlearn the described perverted notions of success and "development" needs to be unlearned for any chance of globally all-inclusive justice with planetary sustainability. Reading that continuously questions how environmental violence sustains the masters' power on the backs of slaves who suffer the most from them is essential. Striving to better understand slave-master power dynamics has no endpoint in ecopedagogical work.

On the opposite side, pedagogically, banking (environmental) teaching models are held tightly by the masters because critical pedagogies, including ecopedagogies, are inherent enemies of their hegemony (Apple, 2004; Gadotti, 1996). I will argue through Freirean tenets that banking pedagogies do not allow for necessary radical transformation for goals of environmental justice and sustainability. This is because the groundings of educational goals are, in part, grounded in these described perverted notions of success, development, and progress. These framings become "commonsense," and challenging them is taught as unthinkable—for example, the perceived abnormal*ness* of not mining natural resources when profiteering is available. Or, possibly, it is seen as "abnormal" to consider environmental devastation outside humans' wants—beyond anthropocentric perspectives. An ecopedagogical question is how can we teach to disrupt neoliberal-based "success" from self-consumption to "success" based on lessening the self's environmental footprint?

Reinvention

Ecopedagogies are reinventions of Freire's work. Reinvention is crucial in bettering our societies, including education, with endless possibilities of becoming more equitable, just, and sustainable. Freire argued that he did not want his work replicated but reinvented location-wise, timewise, experience-wise, culturally, epistemologically, and according to numerous other meaningful contextual aspects. Reinvention coincides with Freire's arguments of needing to teach through reflexivity that humans and our societies are "unfinished," transformative. In other terms, Freire advocated for utopia-based teaching for possibilities of multiple, possible futures. He opposed notions of the world being "finished," condemned to a single, fatalistic future of continuing oppressions, domination, and unsustainability.

There are various Freirean reinventions of environmental pedagogies. In this short-length book, I can only highlight a few key ones. No book of any length or volume of books can be all-inclusive. Freire's arguments that pedagogies should be sociohistorically fluid rather than static have Freireans endlessly reinventing his work. It must be noted that not all reinventions labeled as "Freirean" is genuinely so. I discuss throughout this book the Freirean essence of such reinventions of environmental pedagogies.

Reinvention is also necessary because no single pedagogy or theory can address all socioenvironmental issues. There are many criticisms, some valid and some not, on Freire's lack of focus on social oppressions and environmental dominance (Au & Apple, 2007; McLaren, 2007a, 2007b; Whiting et al., 2018; Misiaszek, 2020), some of which will be discussed in this book.

Freirean Focus of This Book

This book explores Freire's work to reinvent environmental pedagogies by using both his work directly and Freireans' reinventions of his work—including my own as a Freirean. An essential aspect of Freire's work, or any (educational) scholar's work, is that his/her/their scholarship is, to differing degrees, reinventions from others' work—either arguing with or against them. Although the book does not go deeply into Freire's own influences, through which he reinvented his work and his own self, it is important to acknowledge them.

> **Freire's influences:** In *Pedagogy of Hope* (1992), Freire wrote the following list of scholars who "... enlighten the vivid memory that was forming me; Marx, Lukacs, Fromm, Gramsci, Fanon, Memmi, Sartre, Kosik, Agnes Heller, M. Ponty, Simon Weil, Arendt, Marcuse, and so many others" (11). Scholars of Freire have included in the "so many others" that Freire wrote were the following: Hegel, Mannheim, Dewey, Habermas, and Vygotsky, and constructs of French existentialism, Christian personalism, Judeo-Christian anthropology, and liberation theory (Macedo, 2005; Torres, 2014; Mayo, 1999; Morrow & Torres, 2002). Of course, these lists are far from complete.

Other publications that will be coming out in the Bloomsbury *Freire in Focus* series in which this book is housed within will delve into Freire's influences in detail.

Marx was arguably the most substantial influence on Freire, including his ecopedagogical work. If currently alive, he would very likely be doing ecopedagogical work that would coincide, conflict, and reinvent eco-Marxism scholarship and practices being done today. Clark and Foster (2010) argue the following on needing environmental sustainability to be continuously reinvented through Marx's work.

We contend that Marx's materialist and metabolic approach, his emphasis on the contradiction between use value and exchange value and between wealth and accumulation, his focus on sustainable human development, and his critique of capital as a whole, provide an invaluable methodological foundation to critique contemporary environmental degradation and to envision social and ecological transformation. To emphasize the importance of Marx's ecological dialectic is clearly not the same thing as saying that he specifically addressed all of the complex ecological problems that we now confront. (2010, p. 143)

Indirect influences of Marx and others on Freire's work as it relates to constructing ecopedagogies are threaded throughout this book. However, the introductory and condensed nature of this book and the overall series' limits the depth of these discussions. Recognizing Freire's influences is important while reading this book to remember that there are long, diverse histories of constructing critical environmental pedagogies, such as ecopedagogy. This book should be viewed as an introduction to ecopedagogy—a catalyst for increasing scholarship and practices of critical, Freirean environmental scholarship, pedagogical practices, and research that leads toward globally all-inclusive socioenvironmental justice and planetary sustainability. In short, this book should not be viewed as all-inclusive in the topics discussed.

CHAPTER ONE

Freirean Foundations of Environmentalism

The notion seems deplorable to me of engaging in progressive, revolutionary discourse while embracing a practice that negates life—that pollutes the air, the waters, the fields, and devastates forests, destroys the trees and threatens the animals. (Freire, 2004, p. 120)

This chapter introduces the connections between Freire's work and environmental pedagogies. I use his descriptions of Nature, from his early writings in *Pedagogy of the Oppressed* to his later ones, some of which were unfinished due to his untimely death in 1997. I also utilize Freireans' reinventions of environmental pedagogies, that is, ecopedagogies. In personal conversations with Moacir Gadotti, Carlos Alberto Torres, and others, Freire expressed that his next work was to be on ecopedagogy and discussed how *Pedagogy of the Oppressed* was missing a chapter on this topic (Gadotti & Torres, 2009). Consciously avoiding hubris, I wrote with Torres an additional

"Chapter Five" entitled "Ecopedagogy: The Missing Chapter of Pedagogy of the Oppressed" (Misiaszek & Torres, 2019) as if Freire wrote it himself for a new edition of the book.

Freire argued, as his quote indicates, that social and environmental justice cannot be separated in teaching. In essence, Freire connects us (i.e., humans) with the rest of Nature.

> I do not believe in loving among women and men, among human beings, if we do not become capable of loving the world. Ecology has gained tremendous importance at the end of this century. I must be present in any educational practice of a radical, critical, and liberating nature. (Freire, 2004, p. 25)

Freire calls us to teach to love Earth as we (should) love our world. I begin this chapter with the section entitled "world-Earth" to analyze our contested relationships with the rest of Nature in teaching. This chapter ends with unpacking why environmental pedagogies often help to justify unsustainable environmental actions, which sometimes is unintentional. How and why most current environmental pedagogies fail to lead to students' necessary ecological actions outside learning spaces will be discussed.

world-Earth

> A peasant who by banking standards was completely ignorant said: "Now I see that without man there is no world." When the educator responded: "Let's say, for the sake of argument, that all the men on earth were to die, but that the earth itself remained, together with trees, birds, animals, rivers, seas, the stars ... wouldn't all this be a world?" "Oh no," the peasant replied emphatically. "There would be no one to say: This is a world." (Freire, 2000, p. 82)

In our Chapter Five (Misiaszek & Torres, 2019), we referred to Freire's wording of "the world" in the above quote as the anthroposphere—all humans—and "Earth" as the "trees, birds, animals, seas" for reasons previously explained.[1] Freire's exploration of the peasant's response gives a vital example of why the "world" is humans and our interactions. Earth and Nature include the world and all else that makes up the planet.

> **"world-Earth" defined**: The use of the term "world-Earth" emphasizes how our world is *part of* and *inseparable from* Earth. Terminology throughout this book may sometimes seem too "wordy," but English language structures often lead to needed complicated phrases. How language leads to anti-environmentalism is the work of ecolinguistics (Misiaszek, 2021, see Derni, 2008; Fill & Mühlhäusler, 2001). Why I will not objectify Earth by writing "the earth;" why I write "rest of Earth/Nature" or "non-anthroposphere" to indicate the world's inclusion within Earth; and the reasons for the capitalization of Nature have already been ecolinguistically discussed. In addition, "planetary" (including "planetarily" and "planetarism") refer to Earth holistically.

Education that separates and devalues others in the world from the self's private sphere (i.e., "othering") also separates and devalues the rest of Earth as objectified *e*arth and *N*ature as *n*ature. As Freirean reinventions, ecopedagogical work is a "political, awareness-generating task" (Freire, 1993) to understand why anti-environmental acts are done due to learned ideologies that justify them. Unfortunately, there are seemingly endless reasons for false justification, including teaching that *distances* our world from the rest of Nature. Ecopedagogues are tasked to counter such teaching that *distances* "us" from the rest of Earth (Misiaszek, 2012, 2018, 2020c; Misiaszek & Torres, 2019). These tasks include teaching students to read the politics of current and historical world-Earth distancing so that they can point out and unlearn such taught ideologies.

> **"Literacy" defined:** Critical, Freirean literacy education is not solely teaching the mechanics of reading words from a page or a screen. Such technocratic literacy education does not value or even acknowledge students' innate critical reflexivity. Freirean literacy is to read the word to read the World, as will be explained and widened to "read[ing Earth]" throughout this book.

Without using the specific term, the essence of world-Earth de-distancing is what Freire ecopedagogically argued for, that social injustices and the domination of Nature are inseparable (Misiaszek & Torres, 2019; Misiaszek, 2018). I used the somewhat awkward term "anthropo-bio-centric gaps" in previous writings, but it is identical to world-Earth (de-)distancing (see Misiaszek, 2018). Again, it is essential to emphasize that such planetary widening and de-distancing are not absent from Freire's work (Freire, 1993, 1997, 2004).

Reading the world-Earth is neither simple nor easy. It is impossible to understand all the complexities of any social phenomena affecting (anti-)environmentalism worldwide. What is most important to teach is critically problematizing happenings in the world that affect all of Earth. This reading lends itself to endless questioning that, in turn, guides us to what needs to be known next. It is essential to be continuously aware that environmental violence forms continuums, as described earlier. Understanding planetary (un)sustainability is an endless task of balancing with limitless world-Earth contextuality.

Subjective World versus Objective Earth

> There is no historical reality which is not human. There is no history without humankind, and no history for human beings; there is only history of humanity, made by people and (as Marx pointed out) in turn making them. It is when the majorities are denied their right to participate in history as Subjects that they become dominated and alienated. (Freire, 2000, p. 130)

Environmental problem-solving must include deconstructing the local-to-global politics of environmental violence to understand its root causes and local-*to-planetary* effects better. Please note the difference between local-to-*global/planetary* wording to indicate our political world (i.e., *global*) compared with the rest of Nature's apolitical*ness* (i.e., *planetary*). Our world is subjective and transformable, with us being able to (mis)comprehend the rest of Earth as governed by the Laws of Nature (Misiaszek & Torres, 2019; Misiaszek, 2018). Simply put, the rest of Earth will return to a state of equilibrium/balance without reflexivity and will continue to "exist" with or without the world. For example, hurricanes, typhoons, and tornados can be environmentally devastating, but they occur by Nature equaling out air pressure systems rather than motivations of environmental devastation.

> At a certain point in *Capital*, while discussing human work as opposed to other animals, Marx says that a bee could not possibly compare to even the most "modest" of architects. After all, a human being has the capacity for ideating an object before ever producing it. The carpenter has the table drawn up in his or her head before building it. (Freire, 2004, p. 120)

Opposite to the rest of Earth, ecopedagogical work counters notions of our world as objective and finished (i.e., non-transformable). Praxis emergent from reflexivity of world-Earth de-distancing cannot occur in banking (environmental) education models because dominant, hidden ideologies of world-Earth distancing are neither acknowledged nor contested. Returning to the previous example of natural disasters, humans' influence in increasing the frequency and magnitude of hurricanes, typhoons, and tornados from global warming due to human activities is ignored or denied.

Ecopedagogical reading is to better understand Earth holistically through diverse knowledges, perspectives, and epistemologies. Ecopedagogical literacy is unique among other critical literacies in that there are no epistemologies or perspectives outside of our world (or at least known by us yet). This statement does not diminish the valuing of all of Earth in the same way that Freire did not devalue all other animals as some scholars falsely portray (Misiaszek & Torres, 2019; Misiaszek, 2011). Instead, Freire places the burden on humans to be stewards of Earth due to our contextual subjectivity and transformability. This ability allows us to (re)construct the world for planetary sustainability.

Understanding the world's subjectivity is recognizing the politics of the world. Ecopedagogical work includes continuous reflexivity that all knowledges are political, including scientific knowledges, research methodologies, and pedagogical practices (Santos, 2018, 2012; Freire, 1998b, 2000; Harding, 1991, 2006; Figueroa & Harding, 2003; Apple, 2004). Teaching that environmental knowledges are apolitical and neutral inhibits dialogue by silencing students' and others' perspectives on how they make meaning from the knowledges at hand. Neutrality and complete objectivity are impossible in teaching (Freire, 1998b, 2000). For example, absolute objectivity and positivism cannot exist when learning about socioenvironmental oppressions from populations who struggle with them. Such understandings must delve into critically deconstructing the social relations that cause acts that lead to oppressions.

> **"Deconstructing" defined:** Critically deconstructing something is understanding any issue through diverse perspectives with bottom-up approaches that begin with learning oppressions and domination from those who suffer most from environmental violence.

Education is inherently political in curricula selected or not, in how teachers teach, administrations manage education, and various other aspects—all are influenced positively and negatively by local-to-global politics (Freire, 2000; Gadotti, 1996; Apple, 2004).

Globalizations' Contested Terrain

Ecopedagogical work problematizes globalizations as differing processes (de-)distance us from each other and us from the rest of Earth. The plural form of globalizations emphasizes that processes of globalization can either lead to oppressions or empowerment, unsustainability or sustainability (Torres, 2009). The actors of globalization are diverse; Nelly Stromquist (2002), for example, names the following four agents of globalization: the State, transnational corporations (TNCs), mass media, and non-governmental organizations (NGOs). Freire has not been able to witness current intensifying oppressions from globalizations *from above* (i.e., from *globalizers* forced upon *the globalized*) since his unfortunate passing. Nor the possibilities of countering injustices and unsustainability from globalizations *from below* by the globalized. A key example of globalization from above is neoliberal globalization. He wrote the following on globalization theory in one of his last written works below.

Globalization theory, which speaks of ethics, hides the fact that its ethics are those of the marketplace and not the universal ethics of the human person … It is for these matters that we ought to struggle courageously if we have, in truth, made a choice for a humanized world. (Freire, 1998a, p. 114)

Clearly, Freire is speaking of neoliberal globalization rather than globalization *from below,* such as the possibilities for social media to gather support and recognition for environmental justice movements throughout the world. Most of Freire's arguments on globalization focused on denouncing global markets as dehumanizing and without ethics or morality by only prioritizing profiteering to sustain hegemony. It is also deplanetarizing, as Freire argued in his later works (Misiaszek & Torres, 2019), without care for the rest of Earth unless "it" can be commodified. Non-anthropocentric concerns are nil. Although Freire's critiques of globalization are overwhelmingly characterized as oppressive, his focus was on processes from above and, more specifically, neoliberal globalization. I want to emphasize Torres (2009) and other Freirean scholars' arguments that globalizations form contested terrains of negative and positive outcomes.

Teaching to deconstruct economics within ecopedagogical spaces (e.g., spaces of teaching, individual learning, research) is essential, especially the effects of global economics upon local populations and natural environments (Misiaszek, 2018). Freire's ecopedagogical quotes below express the need for education to disrupt global economics for a fatalistic socio-environmental unjust future. The second quote can be read as more planetary in scope and non-anthropocentric in its arguments.

I reject the notion that nothing can be done about the consequences of economic globalization and refuse to bow my head gently because nothing can be done against the unavoidable. Accepting the inexorability of what takes place is an excellent contribution to the dominant forces in their unequal fight against the "condemned of the earth." (Freire, 1997, p. 43)

Their [i.e., global neoliberalists] value system, one where a higher ethic, the one that rules the to-day relations among people, will have been almost completely nonexistent, replaced instead by the ethics of markets, of profit. According to it, people are worth what they make in money every month, and embracing the other, respect for the weaker, a reverence toward life-human, animal, and vegetable—a caring attitude toward things, a taste for beautifulness, the valuing of feelings-all this is reduced to almost no importance or to no importance at all. Although none of that, in my judgment, makes those agents of cruelty any less responsible, the fact in itself that this tragic transgression of ethics has taken place warns us how urgent it is that we fight for more fundamental ethical principles, such as respect for the life of human beings, the life of other animals, of birds, and for the life of rivers and forests. (Freire, 2004, pp. 46–7)

Teaching for ideological acceptance of injustices and unsustainability in the name of economics needs banking (environmental) teaching to instill that a future without prioritizing the global market is impossible.

In fact, the fatalistic discourse which says, "Reality is what it is. What can be done?" declares human impotence and suggests patience and astuteness for better adapting to life as an untouchable reality. Indeed, that discourse is one that sees history as determination. Globalization, such as it is, is inexorable. There is nothing to be done against it, except for waiting, until the very democracy that discourse has been ruining can remake itself, quite magically, in time to detain its destructive effect. (Freire, 2004, p. 117)

Teaching a fatalistic commonsense to accept global oppressions and unsustainability will only lead to these ends.

Opposingly, intensifying globalization has the potential to enrich global collectiveness holistically by deepening and widening equality, equity, diversity, and participatory democracy, all within planetary sustainability. More local-to-global, all-inclusive participation is a grounding tenet of "thick democracy," as opposed to "thin democracy." This is a topic I will delve into more later.

Epistemological Diversity and Decoloniality

Teaching to critically read the epistemologies and positionalities of those affected by environmental violence is essential to more deeply understand their oppressions. As infinitely complex, we need to teach students to understand the world, Nature, and (anti-)environmentalism through diverse epistemologies—"ecologies of knowledges" as termed by Boaventura de Sousa Santos (2018).

Global power dynamics within and between epistemologies legitimize some ways of knowing and delegitimize other ways of knowing. Often, this (de)legitimization coincides with sociohistorical oppressions. Santos (2018) and other critical epistemological scholars would name these "epistemologies of the North," coinciding with the dominance of the global North. Specifically, Santos (2014, 2016, 2018) argues that epistemologies of the North are grounded in coloniality, patriarchy, and capitalism. Thus, education grounded only upon Northern ways of knowing is inherently oppressive. Decolonizing our teaching, knowledges, and epistemologies is essential for all education, including environmental teaching. Decolonizing theories analyze and aid in reinventing environmental teaching for disrupting globalization from above that is, in essence, neocoloniality. Critical decolonizing theories include work from Franz Fanon (1963, 1967), Albert Memmi (1967/1991), and Edward Said's (1979) theories of

Orientalism, among many others. Scholars who work on decolonizing epistemologies include Santos (2014, 2016, 2018) and Raewyn Connell (2007, 2013, 2014) dismiss notions of Northern knowing as apolitical, ahistorical, and unquestionably true. Robert Tierney (2018) argues the need for scholars' teaching to be actively diverse epistemologically as "global meaning makers" for students. This also includes the foci and methodologies of educational research.

Non-dominant epistemologies of the South are opposite to, and inherently oppose, those of the North. Northern-based ideologies have their ways of knowing that are unquestionably "correct," "absolute," and apolitical. As such, other ways of knowing are unnecessary and absurd. Southern epistemologies have diverse ways of knowing as paramount, that is, ecologies of knowledges. Northern devaluing of Southern epistemologies forms barriers, or "limit situations," as Freire named them, to socioenvironmental justice and sustainability.

> **"Limit situations" defined:** "Limit situations consist of contradictions that involve individuals, producing in them an adherence to the facts and, at the same time, leading them to perceive what is happening to them as fatalism. Since they cannot get away from this and do not perceive themselves as being empowered, they accept what is imposed on them, submitting to the events. They are not aware of their submission because the limit situations themselves make each person feel impotent regarding the events in which they are involved." (Osowski, 2012, p. 216)

Teaching through only one dominant epistemological foundation is inherently unjust for both populations whose cultures are rooted upon non-dominant epistemologies and for the world holistically (Santos, 2018; Tierney, 2018; Assié-Lumumba, 2017). Restricting epistemological diversity hampers possibilities for education to help end unsustainable environmental violence.

Santos (2014, 2018) argues for teaching and scholarship to end epistemicide, "destruction of an immense variety of ways of knowing that prevail mainly ... in the colonial societies and sociabilities" (2018). Ecopedagogies innately counter epistemicide—denying all other ways of knowing outside of dominant epistemologies. Acts of epistemicide are limit situations for socioenvironmental justice and sustainability, including utilizing globalizations from above to instill a singular "good" and "legitimate" way(s) of knowing worldwide.

Santos (2014, 2018) uses the term "absences" of academic disciplines to name other ways of knowing beyond dominant epistemologies which are not used. Specifically, his work focuses on "*sociologies of absences.*" Solely teaching through epistemologies of the North further justifies globalizations from above as unconstrained. Marginalized *epistemologies of the South* inherently counter epistemologies of the North's oppressive and unsustainable foundations. I would argue that globalizations from below are crucial for such epistemological disruptions. Disciplinary "emergences" are radical Southern reinventions of disciplines to free them from only Northern foundations. Santos' concepts will be unpacked in this section and throughout the book. However, it is important to note that South/North is not contingent on geographic location but indicates global differing (oppressive) power dynamics.

Unfortunately, better understanding a population's epistemologies can also help to oppress them. Freire warned us about this, stating that "invaders desire to know how those they have invaded apprehend reality-but only so they can dominate the latter more effectively" (Freire, 2000). For example, comparative studies (e.g., comparative and international education (CIE), comparative literacy), sociology, and anthropology have, unfortunately, been used by some as tools of oppression by better knowing those who they dominant and instilling supremacy. An example of this latter aspect of supremacy is CIE benchmarking Western pedagogies to compare all other ways of teaching worldwide; *critical* comparative work inherently counters such scholarship. In other words, gathering knowledges and understanding of the (neo)colonialized is not to better understand them or build ecologies of knowledges, but rather to oppress them further.

Conscientization of the Self's Epistemologies

Ecopedagogues endlessly problem-pose to students how we know what we "know" about the world-Earth, especially "unquestionable" commonsense. Problematizing how our world is understood as (dis)connected from the rest of Earth is an especially important question. For example, Western epistemologies are primarily viewed as world-Earth distancing compared to most Indigenous epistemologies. This often leads to self-reflective questions about what knowledges and ways of knowing have I been taught through (Misiaszek, 2011, 2020b). What are the groundings and histories of these epistemologies? Do I "know" the world-Earth through a single epistemological framing or through multiple, diverse epistemologies? These are some key questions when questioning our and others' epistemological lenses.

Problem-posing aspects of Freirean/ecopedagogical work begin with determining the epistemological commonalities and differences in understanding environmental violence. Ecopedagogical reading requires continuous self-reflexivity on our (anti-)environmental thinking and actions. This reading is often difficult to do because it counters the self's long-held ideologies and epistemological groundings, which are further strengthened when taught in banking education spaces as "how it is"—objectively, neutrally, and absolute. This includes teaching "our" world-Earth perspectives as unquestionably correct and "theirs" as incorrect because they are not "ours." Another difficulty in disrupting our deep-seated commonsense, especially questing our belief that we are free individuals with our "own" individual thoughts. It is especially true for Western individualism. However, we are social beings, and even our most "individual" thoughts have emerged from social interactions (Scherr, 2005); this will be discussed more before the end of this chapter. Yet another difficulty is fear with such self-reflexivity. Freire (2000) discussed that for true conscientization to emerge, fear also emerges from critically questioning deeply-seated understandings of, and the self's positions within, the world-Earth.

We utilize epistemological theories for praxis for ecopedagogical conscientization. For example, Graham Hingangaroa Smith (2000) stresses that we must utilize any and all theories and practices that help to fight against Indigenous struggles (Tierney, 2018). He does not dismiss critically reading any and all epistemologies, theories, and practices but that reading includes possibilities to reinvent them for socioenvironmental justice and sustainability.

Countering Hubris and Anthropocentrism

Disrupting hubris of knowing all the world-Earth and being able to choose the "best" actions always with absolute certainty is an ecopedagogical goal. Absolute knowledge of the world-Earth should be the utopic goal of environmental teaching but with reflexivity that it will never be fully achieved. This utopian goal can be considered a horizon that helps with navigation but cannot be reached (Teodoro & Torres, 2007). The North Star is another good metaphor other scholars have used. Acknowledging these inherent limitations of knowing Earth only through "our" (i.e., humans') perspectives is essential for praxis. There are limitations to trying to understand the world holistically, but it is exponentially more limitations in understanding all of Earth. Understanding the rest of Earth entirely is more complex because we do not "know" what it is not to be "human." In Freirean terms, these are limit situations in environmental teaching, including within ecopedagogies. Recognizing our limits of knowing the complexities of the world-Earth is an essential part of disrupting hubris.

False hubris of "knowing" Earth leads to problematizing various critical questions, including the following. How do our (mis)understandings of Nature lead to environmentally violent acts? How do we view unsustainable violent acts against Nature that we justify? Including how do we justify actions that cause socioenvironmental injustices upon others? I have argued that

> ecopedagogues teach to narrow and ultimately remove the [(i.e., Anthropo-Bio-Centric gap, world-Earth distancing)] … in which praxis for global justice can be achieved, and understood as only achievable, through widened actions for planetary justice. With this, the Freirean limit situations to be discussed in ecopedagogical spaces are the socio-environmental barriers that widen the *Anthropo-Bio-Centric gap* [i.e., world-Earth distancing] for praxis to emerge that overcomes these barriers (i.e., narrowing towards ultimately removing the gap). (Misiaszek, 2018, p. 85)

Problematizing how we have been taught in ways that widen the gap (i.e., world-Earth distancing) that devalue the rest of Nature, especially anthropocentrically when Nature does not benefit humans, is crucial. Limiting epistemologies that we can draw from only increases deplanetarization, especially if epistemologies of the North are the only ones. Critically comparing and contrasting how we understand the world as humans with others is the only way to understand better all of Earth (i.e., de-distancing, narrowing the gap).

It is important to acknowledge that some people exploit notions of limitations of environmental understandings. For example, in our current era of post-truthism, in which perverted teaching of false-truths is rationalized by just touting "we just don't know" and, thus, anything can be "true" (Misiaszek, 2020a). Exploiting the inherent limitations of world-Earth knowing is akin to teaching through lying, as Michael Peters argues on the topic of post-truthism as "government by lying." A good example is climate-change denial with the justification that we "just don't know" everything about the climate and how humans' activities are affecting it or not. Such education lacks truth-seeking goals to indoctrinate instead a false ideology that intensifies hegemony socially constructed in our world (e.g., profit and associated power of fossil fuel industries).

Unfinished, Transformable the World

Uncompleted beings, man is the only one to treat not only his actions but his very self as the object of his reflection; this capacity distinguishes him from the animals, which are unable to separate themselves from their activity and thus are unable to reflect upon it. In this apparently superficial distinction lie the boundaries which delimit the action of each in his life space. Because the animals' activity is an extension of themselves, the results of that activity are also inseparable from themselves: animals can neither set objectives nor infuse their transformation of nature with any significance beyond itself. Moreover, the "decision" to perform this activity belongs not to them but to their species. Animals are, accordingly, fundamentally "beings in themselves. (Freire, 2000, p. 97)

The world is socially constructed by people collectively from deliberate actions; Freire's aim of education is to thicken democratic participation in "re-making" a more just World. This is different from other beings existing without actions emergent from historically reflexive thought. Humans' and societies' unfinishedness, stressed by Freire, allows for transformability (e.g., "development," "progress") guided by our unceasing historical reflectivity and dreaming of possible futures (Freire, 2000).

> Deproblematizing the future, no matter in the name of what, is a breaking away from human nature, which is socially and historically constituted. The future does not make us. We make ourselves in the struggle to make it. (Freire, 2004, p. 34)

Education absent of teaching for possible futures differing from current realities is fatalistically dehumanizing (Freire, 2000). Opposite to the world's inherent unfinishedness is the anthroposphere's finishedness. In other words, transformability does not occur outside the world; the rest of Earth is guided by the Laws of Nature.

Unsustainable environmental violence is from humans' actions that we cognitively determine and, as discussed previously, emerge from our social interactions. Societal structures that help form our decision-making are political, influenced by histories of local-to-global power dynamics. For example, how we may view nature as existing solely for humans' benefits emerges from taught ideologies. Such ideologies often form into thought processes that become "absurd" to question. Teaching to critically problematize such "commonsense" is necessary for socioenvironmental justice and planetary sustainability. Freire termed this "pedagogy of the oppressed," as well as his most famous book, which is (un)consciously teaching ideologies that only further instill oppressions.

Teaching for justice- and sustainability-based praxis focuses on countering such ideologies. Our ability for praxis makes us human; denying praxis, including in teaching, is also dehumanizing (Gadotti, 1996; Freire, 2000).

> The difference between animals—who (because their activity does not constitute limit-acts) cannot create products detached from themselves—and humankind—who through their action upon the world create the realm of culture and history—is that only the latter are beings of the praxis. Only human beings are praxis—the praxis which, as the reflection and action which truly transform reality,

is the source of knowledge and creation. Animal activity, which occurs without a praxis, is not creative; peoples transforming activity is. (Freire, 2000, pp. 100–1)

Teaching for praxis counters pedagogical domestication. Our unique ability to understand the world-Earth through our and others' histories makes praxis possible. Teaching that instills finishedness does not allow for unlearning domestication or learning within pedagogies of the oppressed. When education is perceived as neutral and unchallengeable, this finishedness is instilled as truths, although far from it. Such teaching is also dehumanizing because we are self-reflective, historical beings that can dream of utopias (2000). I would include de-planetarizing here also. It should be noted that Freire's arguments on humans' uniqueness as unfinished, historical beings were influenced, in part, by Fanon's (1963, 1967) theories of decoloniality. Freire significantly edited *Pedagogy of the Oppressed* after reading Fanon's ground-breaking book *Wretched of the Earth* (Schugurensky, 2011).

Freire as anti-environmental?: Some environmental pedagogical scholars argue that Freire placed the rest of Earth outside humans as valueless. I strongly disagree with this argument by referring to Freire's numerous writings after *Pedagogy of the Oppressed* (2000). He further emphasized our unique humanizing factors but stressed this ability as giving us the responsibility to be stewards of all of Earth and condemned the domination of the rest of Nature (McLaren, 2007a, 2007b; Au & Apple, 2007). Our unfinishedness allows us to continuously deepen and widen our understandings of Nature to disrupt unsustainability and oppressions. The Chapter 3 expands on these arguments.

Human unfinishedness is both individual and collective. As humans are social beings (Scherr, 2005), we are not individually constructed inside isolated vacuums but instead socially construct our understandings with others. The self has distinctions, but they are not absolutes. Social constructions of self-individuality largely counter Western concepts of strong individualism as paramount. Arguments frequently arise when, for example, Western-minded persons are told they are not 100 percent their "own person," guided by their absolute individuality. Social constructions of "individuality" also strongly counter neoliberal ideologies of valuing one's self and that individual*ness* and social positionality were due to their actions and intellect.

Development and Unfinishedness

Development emerges from our innate unfinishedness; however, acts of "development" does not necessarily mean positive outcomes for people or planetary sustainability. Perceiving what is "development" is constructed through learned ideologies and can be reconstructed through unlearning ideologies justifying oppressions and unsustainability. It is essential to teach students to ecopedagogically deconstruct if and how justice and planetary well-being factor into our developmental actions' decision-making processes. This includes when we discuss educational goals for sustainable development. Successful sustainability will only occur when long-held ideologies of _D_evelopment are unlearned for, instead, education for _d_evelopment.

_d_evelopment versus _D_evelopment: four defining factors of ... _D_evelopment (capital and italicized '_D_') include the following): (1) neoliberal economics as the sole factor of development analysis; (2) deprioritizing economic justice concern by ignoring how development processes sustain/increase hegemony; (3) deprioritizing planetary sustainability for Earth's balance; and (4) local framings of development are disregarded for globally constructed ones "from above" (e.g., Western _Development_ models), denoted by the lower-case, underlined, and italicized '_d_'. (Misiaszek, 2020c). Ecopedagogues deconstruct non-critical environmental pedagogical models, entirely or in part, to reinvent them to teach widen and deepen literalities to read socioenvironmental actions, including actions for _d/Development._ (Misiaszek, 2020c, p. 16)

Below, Freire (2000) discusses the differences between transformation, adaption, and development.

While all development is transformation, not all transformation is development. The transformation occurring in a seed which under favorable conditions germinates and sprouts, is not development. In the same way, the transformation of an animal is not development. The transformations of seeds and animals are determined by the species to which they belong; and they occur in a time which does not belong to them, for time belongs to humankind … Women and men, among the uncompleted beings, are the only ones which develop. As historical, autobiographical, "beings for themselves," their transformation (development) occurs in their own existential time, never outside it. (Freire, 2000, p. 161)

Ecopedagogical work includes differentiating between "development" and "change" from adaption and evolution. Rather than the term "transformation," I use the word "change." Development occurs from cognitively setting goals. "Change" can be goal-oriented or not, but the word only signifies the mechanics of difference. All development is change, but not all change is development. Development goals can be rooted in furthering or intensifying oppressions, socioenvironmental justices or injustices, anthropocentrism or planetarism, and/or sustainability or unsustainability, among numerous other aspects. Ecopedagogical praxis emerges from deepened and widened reflexivity on these and similar dualities listed. *d*evelopment goals emerge from ecopedagogical praxis and inherently counter actions for *D*evelopment.

Deepened and widened reflectivity for *d*evelopment is impossible within taught ideologies of "development" finished as *D*evelopment because such questioning is "absurd." For example, taught neoliberalism has development outside of economic profiteering as absurd and abnormal. Freire (2000) used various terminologies to explain further these (de)humanizing differences, such as "living" verse "existing" in the phrase "not only live but exist" below, which I would argue are, respectively, "change" versus "development."

In the English language, the terms "live" and "exist" have assumed implications opposite to their etymological origins. As used here, "live" is the more basic term, implying only survival; "exist" implies a deeper involvement in the process of "becoming." (Freire, 2000, p. 98)

Banking education, unfortunately, is a necessary tool for those few who benefit from *D*evelopment in reproducing their hegemony and, in turn, for the masses to "live" rather than "exist." Freire argued that banking education's ideological roots of fatalistic *finishedness* are central tools for sustaining oppressions (Freire, 1992, 1998a, 2000, 2004). Ideologies of finishedness systematically extinguish all possibilities of justice and sustainability outside of current social systems of *D*evelopment. Banking (environmental) education for *D*evelopment structurally limits critical reflexivity, creativity, and curiosity to nil, especially outside of *D*evelopment ideologies, inhibiting ecopedagogical praxis. In short, banking education reproduces oppressive, domineering, and unsustainable _D_evelopment ideologies with teaching that obstructs questioning them. Ecopedagogues teach to identify and counter _D_evelopment ideologies by problem-posing their inseparable connections to unsustainable environmental violence.

_d_evelopment can only emerge from being balanced with the Laws of Nature for planetary sustainability and reflexivity that humans are the only ones challenging Nature's equilibrium/ sustainability. A fundamental conundrum is us being uniquely able to understand our unsustainable actions but also having the ability to decide to do them anyways. This conundrum leads to difficult and complex questioning if we increase our understandings of Nature holistically, will this lead to more sustainable decisions? Will it transform how we view "development?" Ivan Illich (1983) argued that "contemporary [wo]man[/they]" with more scientific knowledge falsely see their anti-environmental actions as without consequence,[2] as opposed to "less-knowledgeable" "classic man" who challenged Nature but understood there would be consequences. Although less knowledgeable about the world-Earth, the latter classic man, Illich argues, is the one who is correct.

Individual and societal unfinishedness allow for constant possibilities of change and transformation; however, them being _d_evelopment or _D_evelopment is the key question. Through the aspects of unfinishedness, Freirean teaching provides utopic ideologies to allow for endless possibilities, but it is not untethered. Utopic _d_evelopment includes not denying others' unfinishedness possibilities, that is, others' _d_evelopment or Earth's sustainability (Misiaszek, 2020b).

Utopia and Realities

Education saturated in utopia, hope, and faith leads students to have imaginaries of better realities and possible actions for achieving them, along with the recognition of current realities. Utopic teaching is, in part, constructing goals to strive for with the recognition that fully achieving them is unlikely, as metaphorically discussed as the horizon or North Star in the previous section. For example, we want to end poverty caused by environmental injustices worldwide. However, the likelihood of ending poverty globally without exception is unlikely. Nevertheless, this does not minimize the need for this goal for ecopedagogical praxis. The United Nations sustainable development goals (SDGs) could be thought of as such utopic goals that are not entirely achievable. Determining the utopic goals is essential for ecopedagogical praxis, along with critical reflexivity on the numerous barriers in reaching the "horizon," that is, limit situations, as named by Freire.

Conscientization of our unfinishedness allows for dreaming of sustainable _d_evelopment possibilities, in conjunction with unlearning goals of fatalistic, unsustainable _D_evelopment.

Critical thinking contrasts with naive thinking, which sees "historical time as a weight, a stratification of the acquisitions and experiences of the past," from which the present should emerge "normalized" and "well-behaved." (Freire, 2000, p. 92)

Freire argued that our histories construct our futures; however, he did not mean this in fatalistic ways. Freire (2004) expressed this below by using the metaphor of building a wall in which "tomorrow" does not have to be a repetition of "today" or yesterday, but that it is a brick in the wall nonetheless.

My refusal to understand history as a determination) thus, my rejection of an inexorable tomorrow. Tomorrow is neither a necessary repetition of today, as the dominant would like it to be, nor something predetermined. Tomorrow is a possibility we need to work out and, above all, one we must fight to build. What takes place today does not inevitably produce a tomorrow. (Freire, 2004, p. 75)

Reinventing his words within the ecopedagogical term of d/Development, ecopedagogues teach by problematizing *what* we are progressing toward—brick-by-brick, in the metaphor—to "produce a tomorrow." Ecopedagogical sociohistorical analysis is accomplished by understanding that critically reading the past is essential for today's and tomorrow's praxis to cease histories of oppressions and unsustainability.

Utopia within education is grounded in reality, including the realities of environmental devastation, unsustainability, and socioenvironmental suffering. Utopic teaching for development includes problem-posing the limitations of "our" unfinishedness within the rest of Earth's finishedness. In other words, our subjectivity within the rest of Earth guided by the Laws of Nature.

> Problem-posing education affirms men and women as beings in the process of becoming—as unfinished, uncompleted beings in and with a likewise unfinished reality. Indeed, in contrast to other animals who are unfinished, but not historical, people know themselves to be unfinished; they are aware of their incompletion. In this incompletion and this awareness lie the very roots of education as an exclusively human manifestation. The unfinished character of human beings and the transformational character of reality necessitate that education be an ongoing activity. (Freire, 2000, p. 84)

Teaching for development as utopic goals must be within the realities of planetary sustainability and does not result in others' oppressions. The "transformational character of reality" that Freire speaks of also has Nature's limitations to reality. This includes deconstructing our sociohistorical relationships that have, and continue to, misguide the utilization of Earth's resources to fulfill "our" dreams but also result in "their" nightmares.

Freire (2000) wrote the following on praxis emergent from rigorous critical deconstruction of realities through deepened and widened reflexivity.

People will be truly critical if they live the plenitude of the praxis, that is, if their action encompasses a critical reflection which increasingly organizes their thinking and thus leads them to move from a purely naive knowledge of reality to a higher level, one which enables them to perceive the causes of reality. (Freire, 2000, p. 131)

Above, Freire describes a building up of deepening and widening understandings of realities to guide actions (i.e., praxis). "Plenitude of the praxis" cannot occur within fatalistic banking education models because the teaching defines it as impossible, reproducing a destined singular future of injustices and unsustainability. In short, banking education obscures realities and is absent of dreaming of possible better, just, and sustainable futures.

Fatalism of Globalization from Above

If my presence in history is not neutral, I must accept its political nature as critically as possible. If, in reality, I am not in the world simply to adapt to it, but rather to transform it, and if it is not possible to change the world without a certain dream or vision for it, I must make use of every possibility there is not only to speak about my utopia, but also to engage in practices consistent with it. (Freire, 2004, p. 7)

Deconstructing global influences of instilling fatalism is essential in ecopedagogies, including fatalism emergent from (environmental) education. Freire (2000) argued that fatalism is intensified by globalization from above by having "hope" guided, limited, and measured by neoliberal "success," as discussed previously. Neoliberal globalization's influences on eradicating utopia from education are described by Freire (2004) below.

If there are no social classes any longer, and if their conflicts are gone as well; if there is no ideology any longer, from left or right; if economic globalization has not only made the world smaller but made it almost equal, the education needed today has nothing to do with dreams, utopias, or conscientização (the building of critical awareness and conscience). In that view, education has nothing to do with ideologies) but rather with technical knowledge. (Freire, 2004, p. 78)

His description tells how neoliberalism and hegemony are sustained by having technocratic, domesticating training that increases oppressors' profiteering through the labor of the oppressed. In addition, such training lacks teaching the transformational tools to fight against oppressions. Such fatalistic *training* without critical *education* only gives "hope" to profiteering hegemonic actors.

As seen in Freire's (1998a) quote below, such training must have its neoliberal goals hidden, including who truly are the "oppressors" and the "oppressed."

Globalization is inevitable. Nothing can be done about it. It must happen because, mysteriously, that is how destiny has arranged things. So, we must accept what in essence only strengthens the control by powerful elites and fragments and pulverizes the power of the marginalized, making them even more impotent. Prisoners of fate. There is nothing left to do except bow our heads humbly and thank God that we are still alive. Thank God. And perhaps globalization too. I have always rejected fatalism. I prefer rebelliousness because it affirms my status as a person who has never given in to the manipulations and strategies designed to reduce the human person to nothing. The recently proclaimed death of history, which symbolizes the death of utopia, of our right to dream, reinforces without doubt the claims that imprison our freedom. This makes the struggle for the restoration of utopia all the more necessary. (Freire, 1998a, pp. 102–3)

Hope within neoliberal globalization is pure survival for the masses rather than living. The rest of Nature becomes commodified objects. Freire expresses that teaching through fatalism, and the loss of one's history opposes the self's innate freedom and, thus, dehumanizing. It is deplanetarizing as well. Physically being still "alive" does not equate to "living," with globalizations that further "fragments and pulverizes the power of the marginalized, making them even more impotent." Freire (2000) discussed the dehumanizing aspects of silencing the othered by systematically removing them from history.

> There is no historical reality which is not human. There is no history without humankind, and no history for human beings; there is only history of humanity, made by people and (as Marx pointed out) in turn making them. It is when the majorities are denied their right to participate in history as Subjects that they become dominated and alienated. (Freire, 2000, p. 130)

What Freire states above coincides with Memmi's (1991) argument that one of the colonizers' most oppressive actions was structurally eliminating the colonized's histories. Freire (1992, 2000) expressed how banking education objectifies students to not being active Subjects in their own histories and, in turn, instills fatalism (i.e., being objects of *others'* histories rather than active participants in *their* possible futures). Taking away the "right to participate in history as Subjects" and being able to construct possible futures invalidates and justifies histories and a dictated future of suffering from environmental violence.

Sustainability Baselines

There are world-Earth sustainability balancing points; however, our determining them can differ from *actual* ones dictated by the Laws for Nature. "What is the baseline(s) of sustainability?" is a question that must be continuously problematized. Such problematizing is incredibly complex and calls for endless learning. This is especially true in an increasingly globalized world with unbalanced _Development practices dictated by neoliberalism that has us accelerating away from a true sustainability baseline (Misiaszek, 2020d) (see Rosa, 2003; Moore, 2017). But it is also complicated by balancing environmental justice in the world and sustainability for the rest of Earth. For example, a more equitable distribution of natural resources globally can lead to sustainability within the world but does <u>not</u> necessarily correspond to Earth's balance or limitations. In other words, achieving sustainability in the world, even with equity and social justice, does not necessarily equate to planetary sustainability.

If we benchmark today's world as the baseline, present socioenvironmental injustices and devastation will only continue at current levels (Misiaszek, 2020b; Misiaszek, 2018). Instead, narrowing the gap between false sustainability baselines and Earth's true balancing point is crucial. For example, if the sustainability baseline is set at current levels, while I am writing this in 2021, global warming will unquestionably only intensify. I write this in the hope that global warming is diminishing when you read this sentence. Unfortunately, we are already at, or over, the tipping point in needing to eliminate fossil fuel usage. Logically, this fact should dictate how we define the sustainability baseline and illustrate the urgency of changing our energy sources. However, _Development counters such rationale with neoliberal illogicalness and its prevalence due to globalizations.

Banking Environmental Pedagogies' Failures

I have already discussed some crucial ways banking environmental pedagogies fail; this section will delve more into the details and Freirean reasonings for their failures. Countering shallow banking environmental teaching is essential because they are frequently more environmentally harmful than if the teaching never occurred (Misiaszek, 2011, 2015, 2018). My argument here may initially seem counterintuitive. However, schooling, as Apple (Apple, 2004, 2006) argues, is most powerful at instilling ideologies the earlier they are "taught" to students (i.e., best at younger ages). Ecopedagogical work includes unveiling and disrupting banking environmental pedagogies in research, learning, and literacies learned.

Banking educators view their students "in the world" by:

Assum[ing] ... a dichotomy between human beings and the world: a person is merely in the world, not with the world or with others; the individual is spectator, not re-creator." (Freire, 2000, p. 175)

Ecopedagogically reinventing Freire's quote above, students are viewed as *on* the *e*arth (purposely objectified with the lowercased "earth" and the "the") rather than *with E*arth and *part of E*arth. Banking environmental teaching extends the outsider*ness* and objectification of students from the rest of the world and Earth, as opposed to students being Subjects within the world-Earth. Ecopedagogical praxis cannot emerge from banking models because ideologies are taught as unchallengeable even if they result in oppressions and unsustainability. Students are mere objects to meekly adapt to their education, the world, and Earth rather than subjective, agents of transformation. Students are to be taught *at* to avoid classroom dialogue that includes their thoughts on the necessary actions to end oppressions and unsustainability.

Educators perceive themselves as the sole knowledge holders within banking spaces, with "knowledge [a]s a gift bestowed by those who consider themselves knowledgeable [i.e., teachers] upon those whom they consider to know nothing [i.e., students]" (Freire, 2000). Banking systems determine "worthy" knowledges, epistemologies, and teaching practices, as well as the curricula from these selections, without students' input. All this decision-making is veiled in false neutrality; thus, questioning what is being taught is foolhardy. "Official" knowledges are not challenged in learning spaces, silencing all voices other than the teacher's. Apple (2004) argues that critical educators must problematize what is *not* in the curricula and why, as much as analyze what is in the curricula.

Banking education, at best, does not support, and at worst counters, students' environmental praxis. Students' praxis is not impossible if taught within banking spaces because not all learning happens within formal learning spaces (Apple, 2004). Teaching through banking approaches has students being forced to critically question what they are learning outside of formal education spaces. Freire argues that students must maintain "flame[s] of resistance" against their banking teaching experiences.

> What is essential is that learners, though subjected to the praxis of the "banking system," maintain alive the flame of resistance that sharpens their curiosity and stimulates their capacity for risk, for adventure, so as to immunize themselves against the banking system. (Freire, 1998a, p. 33)

Schooling is an important factor in students' learning and ideological construction; however, students can and do rebel in various constructive ways against what they are taught. For banking education to continue with lease resistance, such rebellion must be systematically stamped out—such "flames" must be extinguished. "Successful" environmental banking teaching, which "regards men as adaptable, manageable beings" (Freire, 2000), has the perverted goal of making students "adaptable" to environmental harm placed upon them and others. Thus, this perverted logic has socioenvironmental oppressions to be expected, and countering them is frequently unnecessary and foolish.

Banking education "minimize[s] or annul[s] the student's creative power" (Freire, 2000) to suffocate flames of possible praxis. Such teaching reduces "being environmental" to superficially knowing ecological issues without recognizing their capacity to be agents of environmental transformation. Students are taught to be objects of a predetermined future by both mystifying and teaching them to accept a horrible fate.

> Domination is itself objectively divisive. It maintains the oppressed in a position of "adhesion" to a reality which seems all powerful and overwhelming, and then alienates by presenting mysterious forces to explain this power. (Freire, 2000, p. 173)

Hegemonic actors who most benefit from unsustainable environmental violence rely on mystifying the "realities" of the resulting injustices and devastation from the violence. False realities that support hegemony are apolitically taught as "just how it is." This teaching justifies and denies local-to-global power dynamics of why violence occurs and inequalities of suffering.

Neoliberal Oppressions, Dominance, and Unsustainability

> Oppressors develop the conviction that it is possible for them to transform everything into objects of their purchasing power; hence their strictly materialistic concept of existence. Money is the measure of all things, and profit the primary goal. For the oppressors, what is worthwhile is to have more—always more—even at the cost of the oppressed having less or having nothing. For them, *to be is to have* and to be the class of the "haves." (Freire, 2000, p. 58, emphasis in original)

As discussed already and emphasized in his quote above, Freire despised neoliberalism and its global proliferation. I introduce neoliberalism to students as an ideology that has everything boiled down to economic profiteering for the self and their private sphere. For example, this includes all educational, health, and environmental issues being simplified to questions of economic gains and losses, while also systematically hiding all the associated local-to-global power dynamics. This includes neoliberalism's saturation into all aspects of (anti-)environmental teaching.

Neoliberalism is grounded in sustaining and intensifying hegemony rather than widespread economic justice. For neoliberalism to succeed, education must first veil its hegemonic goals and have false, hidden curricula that everyone will profit from and benefit from adhering to its tenets (Apple, 1999). Teaching must also normalize neoliberalism by entrenching the lie that all other economic models are impossible, perverted, and abnormal.

Freire's metaphor of "jumping on the train" below indicates that neoliberalism is not intended for the passengers (i.e., the masse) to profit economically but for hegemonic actors to profit and increase their control.

> [Considering to adhering to global neoliberal is] a question of jumping on the train in the middle of the journey without discussing the conditions, the cultures, or the forms of production of the countries that are being swept along. And there is no talk about the distance that separates the "rights" of the strong and their power to enjoy them from the fragility of the weak in their attempts to exercise their rights. Meanwhile, responsibilities and duties are leveled-equal for all. If globalization means the abolition of the frontiers and the opening without restriction to free enterprise, those who cannot compete simply disappear. (Freire, 1998a, pp. 113–14)

Having people board the train is done through falsely teaching them that they will only benefit from neoliberalism, and it is the only train running (i.e., the only "viable" economic system). Teaching for conscientization that this is not true is an ecopedagogical goal. Perverted faith in neoliberalism within the global market is dehumanizing and deplanetarizing.

> Mechanists and humanists alike recognize the power of today's globalized economy. However, while for the former there is nothing to be done about this untouchable power, for the latter, it is not only possible but also necessary to fight against the robust power of the powerful, which globalization has intensified, as it has the weakness of the fragile. If economic structures indeed dominate me in such a masterful manner as to shape my thinking, to make me a docile object of their power, how can I explain political struggle, and above all, how can struggle be undertaken and in the name of what? ... To me, it should be undertaken in the name of ethics, obviously not the ethics of markets but rather the universal ethics of human beings—in the name of the needed transformation of society that should result in overcoming dehumanizing injustice. (Freire, 2004, p. 35)

Freire passionately argued for the resistance to neoliberalism seeping into all facets of education, from the ideologies being learned to pedagogical selection to educational administration, research on education, and everything in between.

Ecopedagogues teach through lenses that are "not impartial or objective" to human suffering and Nature's destruction, including due to neoliberalism.

> I cannot avoid a permanently critical attitude toward what I consider to be the scourge of neoliberalism, with its cynical fatalism and its inflexible negation of the right to dream differently, to dream of utopia. My abhorrence of neoliberalism helps to explain my legitimate anger when I speak of the injustices to which the ragpickers among humanity are condemned. ... I am not impartial or objective; not a fixed observer of facts and happenings. I never was able to be an adherent of the traits that falsely claim impartiality or objectivity. That did not prevent me,

however, from holding always a rigorously ethical position. (Freire, 1998a, p. 22)

Ecopedagogues cannot be, nor teach students to be, "fixed observer[s] of facts and happenings" (Freire, 1998a) of oppression and domination without having countering actions (Misiaszek, 2020b). Teaching to identify, counter, and radically reinvent teaching entrenched in neoliberalism is the goal of Freireans and, in turn, ecopedagogues. Neoliberal teaching of valuing through economics without socioenvironmental justice, sustainability, and peace will only lead toward opposite, devastating outcomes.

CHAPTER TWO

Ecopedagogical Teaching

Describing the key aspects of ecopedagogical practices will be this chapter's focus. In these discussions, I will continue to compare ecopedagogies to other environmental pedagogical models.

Ecopedagogical Literacy

Ecopedagogical literacy is the ability to read for *deepened* understandings of more localized, contextual causes and effects of environmental violence, *widened* understandings from others' perspectives beyond the self-defined local and effects upon Nature beyond humans, and the intersectionalities between them (Misiaszek & Torres, 2019; Misiaszek, 2018, 2020b).

> What does not seem possible to me is to read the word without a connection to the learners reading of the world. That is why, for me, the literacy process with adults necessarily implies the critical development of the reading of the world, which is a political, awareness-generating task. What would be wrong, and what I have never suggested

should be done, is to deny learners their right to literacy because of the necessary politicization there would not be time for literacy in the strict sense of the term. Literacy involves not just the reading of the word, but also the reading of the world. (Freire, 1993, pp. 58–9)

Ecopedagogical literacy is discussed throughout this book's chapters as teaching students to critically read the world as part of Earth. Freire emphasized this planetary aspect in the above quote and throughout his later work. This aspect defines the focus of ecopedagogy. It is not that Freirean pedagogies are absent of environmentalism, but rather ecopedagogues focus on teaching literacy toward ending oppressions and domination from how the world treats the rest of Nature.

In critical literacy terminology, reading the politics that influence education to justify unsustainable environmental violence and unveil the actual costs to humanity and Earth wholistically. Reading includes how environmental violence affects populations unequally, such as by race, ethnicity, gender, socioeconomics, sexual orientation, and global South/North positioning. Teaching to critically read environmental oppressions aligning with historical oppressions is too frequently absent from classrooms as they are deemed too "politically sensitive" or "uncomfortable" topics. Such rationale only weakens literacy for gaining environmental understandings crucial for transformation. In addition, ecopedagogical literacy focuses on reading the effects of violence upon the non-anthroposphere beyond humans' interests. Such reading requires, in part, the disruption of anthropocentric ideologies, including neoliberalism, which devalues, objectifies, and commodifies Nature outside of humans (Misiaszek, 2011, 2020b, 2020c).

Ecopedagogical literacy is essential for learning oppressions *from* those who struggle from them. Gadotti (1996) argued through Freire's work that praxis can only occur in such bottom-up approaches. Opposingly, banking pedagogues silence the voices of the "bottom" for only "authoritative" voices to be heard. These voices frequently justify unsustainable environmental violence. Also, anthropocentric indoctrination diminishes the caring for the rest of Nature toward nil.

Dialogue

> Speaking their word that people, by naming the world, transform it, dialogue imposes itself as the way by which they achieve significance as human beings. (Freire, 2000, p. 88)

As already discussed through Freire's work, *ecopedagogical spaces* are democratic and dialectic. Being "democratic" is significant and meaningful inclusion of knowledges, experiences, and epistemologies of all those within learning spaces. Dialogical learning spaces have teachers and students share and truly listen to everyone's knowledges, experiences, and perspectives as everyone teaches and learns together.

> The teacher-of-the-students and the students-of-the-teacher cease to exist and a new term emerges: teacher-student with students-teachers. The teacher is no longer merely the-one-who-teaches, but one who is himself taught in dialogue with the students, who in turn while being taught also teach. (Freire, 2000, p. 80)

As education emerges from the realities outside the classroom walls (either tangibly or figuratively), ecopedagogical dialogue emerges from local realities which are meaningful to those in the classroom. This does not limit learning to only local aspects, realities, meanings, and ways of knowing, but that teaching is *through* them.

Listening is essential for dialectical teaching. Freirean dialogue is not a debate to win but to listen and respond together to further deepen and widen everyone's understandings together. Constructive dialectic conflict cannot occur if students and teachers are fixated on winning arguments than trying to understand each other's knowledges and questions on the topic at hand.

Teaching and learning through critical dialogue connects one's own realities through better understanding and respecting others' understandings and realities. In addition, critical dialogue allows for better critical understandings of one's own self, current limitations of our understanding, and what needs to be learned next. Freire (1997, 2000) also discussed the need for "love" for one another within dialectic spaces and including others' understandings outside the learning space into the dialogue. Analyzing self-reflexivity lends itself to the classic methodological question of what are the "best" perspective(s) to understand a fish swimming in a bowl? Is it better from the fish's perspectives (e.g., participatory research) or as an outside observer looking at the fishbowl? Both perspectives are necessary to understand better what is happening in the bowl, critically comparing the commonalities and differences between the fish's and the observer's perspectives. Limitations of "knowing" from outside-the-self's positionalities will be discussed later in the chapter.

Conversely, top-bottom approaches that instill intellectual elitism devalue all "other" knowledges. Outside truth-seeking knowing should be utilized but must be incorporated democratically and dialectically, as opposed to being forced upon them as mystified, superior knowledges which belittles all other ways of knowing. Within ecopedagogical terms used previously, such learning *widens* students' knowing others globally and Earth planetarily, and *deepens* their understanding of themselves and their self-defined Local.

Santos (2018), among others, argues that self-reflection confined singularly to one's own epistemologies only helps to reproduce rather than counter injustices and unsustainability. Reproduction is especially harmful when epistemologies are grounded within sociohistorical oppressions (e.g., *epistemologies of the North*) and globalizations that further entrenches them worldwide. Ecopedagogical dialogue includes problematizing what is perceived as *known* of the world-Earth—"the underlying epistemological and ideological assumptions that are made about what counts as 'official' or legitimate knowledge and who holds it" (Apple & Au, 2009; Apple, 2000, 2004). Diversity in dialectical teaching helps to construct self-reflexivity to learn oppressions *through* the eyes of those who suffer the most (Gadotti, 1996), as well as selectively using or countering foreign knowledges, ways of knowing, and theories.

Authentic Dialogue and Conflict

Teaching by having students voiceless and unable to participate in their education is dehumanizing. Being "voiceless" is not necessarily students not being able to utter words but not being able to authentically discuss what is being taught.

> Cooperation leads dialogical Subjects to focus their attention on the reality which mediates them and which-posed as a problem-challenges them. The response to that challenge is the action of dialogical Subjects upon reality in order to transform it. Let me reemphasize that posing reality as a problem does not mean sloganizing: it means critical analysis of a problematic reality. (Freire, 2000, p. 168)

Authentic dialogue can only occur in ecopedagogical spaces where everyone feels safe to discuss and actively listen to each other's deepened and widened understandings, experiences, and epistemological perspectives of environmental issues. Authenticity of dialogue is the freedom of speaking one's mind rather than pleasing the teacher and other students, as well as speaking meaningfully (e.g., not "sloganizing").

Freire (2000) gave the following tenets of authentic dialogue:

- *Right for everyone*
- *False words* are non-transformable

- speaking their word that people, by naming the world, transform it, dialogue imposes itself as the way by which they achieve significance as human beings (p. 88)

- Making meaning as essential/not "deposited"

He argued that "dialogue with the people is neither a concession nor a gift, much less a tactic to be used for domination" (Freire, 2000).

Difficulties and frustrations will surely emerge from the dialogue. One source will be from a sense of fatalism that the world is not transformable that has been instilled through students' many years of banking education that silences them and dismisses possibilities of praxis. Banking education isolates students from their own and others' realities, thus not getting the chance to better understand their own realities through others' experiences and perspectives.

Education as the practice of freedom—as opposed to education as the practice of domination—denies that man is abstract, isolated, independent and unattached to the world; it also denies that the world exists as a reality apart from people. (Freire, 2000, p. 81)

The goal of needing conflict-free learning spaces is false and detrimental to learning (Freire, 1998b, 2000; Apple, 2004).

Banking techniques of separation and isolation deny students collective constructions of questioning environmental violence for praxis.

Thinking that is concerned about reality, does not take place in ivory tower isolation, but only in communication. If it is true that thought has meaning only when generated by action upon the world, the subordination of students to teachers becomes impossible. (Freire, 2000, p. 77)

In banking spaces, students' realities are denied beyond what is spoon-fed to them as "reality."

Conflict will always emerge from authentic dialogue because we often have opposing ways of understanding the world-Earth. Within ecopedagogical spaces, conflict is necessary and, as Freire (2000) argued, makes us human.

> Authentic adherence is the free coincidence of choices; it cannot occur apart from communication among people, mediated by reality. (Freire, 2000, p. 168)

Below, I express the need for dialogical conflict in ecopedagogical teaching in terms of "development," in which

> democracy depends on differences, dissonance, conflict, and antagonism, so that deliberation is radically indeterminate (Jickling & Wals, 2008; Goodman & Saltman, 2002; Saul, 1995). All environmental pedagogies will inevitably encounter these conflicts, but the difference in ecopedagogies is that conflicts are beyond not ignored, but that teaching is grounded at these points of tension, especially in the deconstruction of developments for the term's reconstruction that is within socioenvironmental models. (Misiaszek, 2018, p. 159)

Conflict-free dialogue on the topic of (sustainable) development is impossible in teaching and can only promote education for _D_evelopment rather than for _d_evelopment.

Freire discussed how democracy must guide development rather than the other way around in his "talking book" with Myles Horton (1990a), civil rights leader and educator from Appalachia, United States.

> Freire: The more people participate in the process of their own education, the more the people participate in the process of defining what kind of production to produce, and for what and why, the more the people participate in the development of their selves. The more the people become themselves, the better the democracy. (Horton, 1990a, p. 145)

The phrase "development of their selves" is not touting neoliberal individualism, but rather the self as *part of* society toward "becoming themselves" collectively. Emphasized here is the need for students' "participat[ion]" by having classrooms saturated in democratic, authentic dialogue, and emergent conflict is embraced rather than avoided.

Conundrums and Tensions

One conundrum is that ecopedagogues have the inherent goal of their students partaking in environmental actions through praxis, but this does not mean this will happen for all students. It is inevitable that diverse outcomes will emerge from authentic dialogue in ecopedagogical spaces. Some students will likely not emerge as our ideal "environmentalists" or possibly even become more anti-environmental after we teach them.

Creating safe spaces requires constant reflexivity and self-constraint in the fact that students have the freedom of becoming "environmental" or not. Safe spaces are "free from violence (e.g., verbal, mental, physical, emotional) are essential for student(s)-student(s) and student(s)-teacher(s) conflicts on socioenvironmental issues" (Misiaszek, 2020c). For example, what if some students who were climate change deniers remain deniers after taking ecopedagogical courses? Freirean pedagogues do not teach students what to think but help them to think critically through deepened and widened understandings for (re)constructing their understandings.

> [the] object of dialogical-libertarian action is not to "dislodge" the oppressed from a mythological reality in order to "bind" them to another reality. On the contrary, the object of dialogical action is to make it possible for the oppressed, by perceiving their adhesion, to opt to transform an unjust reality (away from cultural invasion). (Freire, 2000, p. 174)

Ecopedagogical work has the goals given in this paragraph's first sentence; however, achieving them should not lead to banking teaching. Ecopedagogues need to work out such tensions contextually. My own experiences have had both successes and failures in rectifying these tensions.

Respecting and valuing diverse perspectives within learning spaces includes dealing with students countering environmentalism held dearly by ecopedagogues. Freire argues below that we should not teach students what to think, as banking educators do, but rather how to understand the world (or the world-Earth) better critically through diverse perspectives.

> Not our role to speak to the people about our own view of the world, nor to attempt to impose that view on them, but rather to dialogue with the people about their view and ours. (Freire, 2000, p. 96)

Freire (1998a, 2000a) emphasized that apolitical education is impossible, which includes tensions that arise when students challenge teachers' deep-seated ideologies, values, and ethics. For example, environmental ones. These tensions coincide with tensions outside of classrooms. I often ask my students that if our classrooms cannot have such conflictive and authentic dialogue peacefully and constructively, how can we expect dialogue in the world, with its infinite diversity, to lead to environmentalism? However, Freirean pedagogy is not value-free (Harding, 1991); it is not extreme postmodernism in which everything, including suffering, is relational. There is real suffering, and there is real environmental devastation. Ecopedagogy does not adhere to, for example, Hayden White's (1973) theory that all history is fiction—there have been real sociohistorical oppressions that caused, and continue to cause, suffering and unsustainability. Freire argued that our "free coincidence of choices cannot occur apart from communication among people, mediated by reality" (Freire, 2000). The art of ecopedagogical teaching is balancing authentic dialogue and socioenvironmental realities.

Ecopedagogical work is truth-seeking *within* socioenvironmental realities, which, in turn, innately disrupts fictional anti-environmental post-truthism (Misiaszek, 2020a). Post-truthers are ignorant of, or purposely ignore, these reality-based foundations when arguing that post-truthism is just utilizing critical theories' subjectivity to question knowledges (Peters et al., 2018). Anti-environmental false-truths, sometimes portrayed deceptively as "environmental" ones, are taught as purposeful lies for "them" to benefit. One of the most prominent examples of this is climate change denial. Without authentic dialogue in environmental teaching spaces, the possibilities of challenging false-truths touted inside and/ or outside the spaces are very limited. Dialectic spaces are increasingly needed as post-truthism is further entrenched in our current world.

Aligning with Foucault, Habermas, and other scholars' arguments on dialectics, dialogue on environmentalism cannot occur without jointly agreed upon world-Earth truths (Misiaszek, 2020a). In other words, all dialogue needs some mutual agreements; however, post-truthism removes any agreements about what is true or false. For example, discussions on whether to invest in space travel require the truth that travel is possible around Earth that is spherical in shape. Post-truth arguments that the Earth is flat do not allow for any constructive discussions on answering this question. Another example is that Earth's temperature is not warming because somewhere globally, it snowed. This falsity does not lead to a critical dialogue on global warming issues. Post-truthism leads people to further entrench their beliefs in false-truths by not listening to evidence or others' perspectives; arguing with environmental "information" they found on the internet that coincides with their opinions and ideologies (Misiaszek, 2020a). I often challenge my students to say any crazy idea, and I bet them I can find someone online that agrees the idea is true.

Another conundrum is hypocrisy. Self-reflexivity of our actions can conflict with ideals held by ecopedagogues and environmentalists. Some hypocritical questions might include the following: Do I eat meat? Do we take hot, long showers? and do we travel long distances that require environmentally harmful plane flights? Unquestionably, I have found myself being a hypocrite within these and numerous other examples daily, questioning my actions, positionalities, identities, and confidence in achieving praxis. There are no easy answers to overcoming these conundrums. However, I return to Freirean tenets of requiring safe spaces for authentic dialogue on the conflicts and hypocrisies of "being" environmental to, in part, counter these and other conundrums.

Authority versus Authoritarianism

Some people argue that critical/Freirean pedagogies take away teachers' authority. Although critical pedagogies do inherently dissolve authoritarian teaching and teacher–student hierarchies, teachers still have authority in formal learning spaces.

> Authentic authority is not affirmed as such by a mere transfer of power, but through delegation or in sympathetic adherence. If authority is merely transferred from one group to another, or is imposed upon the majority, it degenerates into authoritarianism. (Freire, 2000, p. 178)

Learning is not only from the teacher in an authoritarian manner, but students also learn from each other, and teachers learn from them also. Outside teaching resources (e.g., books, textbooks, videos) are brought into ecopedagogical spaces; however, resources are not taught as unquestionable or cannot be reinvented (Horton et al., 1990a). This also includes outside lecturers labeled as "experts." Horton (1990b) goes as far as to emphasize that invited "experts" should be democratically determined by everyone in the learning space, and they should be *part of* the democratic dialogue rather than talking/teaching *at* students.

Another misconception is that Freirean teaching is without lecturing. Ecopedagogues still lecture in classrooms but not *only* lecture. They also, for example, facilitate and contribute to democratic classroom dialogue and adjust their lectures according to the discussions. There are also tensions with education's goals and its traditional terminology. In their talking book (1990a), Freire discussed with Horton how sometimes calling a teacher a "teacher" is somewhat erroneous for critical teaching.

> Freire: Instead of naming a school for adults, I named the space and the students and the teacher "Circle of Culture" in order to avoid a name that sounds to me too much like traditional school. Instead of calling the teacher "teacher," I named him or her "coordinator of discussion, of debate, dialogue." And the students I called "participants of discussion." (Horton et al., 1990a, p. 84)

Later Horton talked about how his Highlander Education and Research Center was not an organizers' training school but an educational space.

> Horton: [people] assumed that we were an organizer's training school. But I kept saying no, no. We do education and they become organized. They become officials. Basically it's not technical training. We're not in the technical business. We emphasize ways you analyze and perform and relate to people, but that's what I call education, not organizing. (Horton et al., 1990a, pp. 115–16)

Both Horton and Freire talk about the contested politics of environmental educators teaching to produce environmentalists. Freire avoided traditional schooling terms, and Horton emphasized the differences between organizational training and education. For Horton (Horton et al., 1990a, 1990b), organizations(ers) "push" ideologies for direct action as compared to critical educators who teach students to construct their own world-Earth understandings, ways of knowing, and ideological formations collectively and individually. Unlike training for environmental justice organizations, ecopedagogues' desired learning outcomes are not so pragmatically focused upon. Rather, they also focus on the pathways *toward* students becoming environmentalists and acting as such. This does not devalue organizations' work but highlights some key differences between the two.

CHAPTER THREE

Curricula through Generative Themes

The quality of ecopedagogical teaching does not equate to the amount of didactic information taught. Instead, it is measured by the deepening and widening of socioenvironmental understandings gained and the ability to read to gain such understandings outside of classrooms. This goal counters many (environmental) pedagogical models based on the quantity of knowledge deposited. This includes a neoliberal educational assessment with testing of didactic information that is seemingly endless.

Coinciding with critical pedagogues who oppose static, predetermined curricula (Freire, 2000; Apple, 2004), ecopedagogues co-construct syllabi with students on how course topics will be taught. Curricula are diverse in definition, but here, I am referring to the resources and ways in which topics are taught. Michael Apple (2004) argues that problematizing curricula includes asking what is *not* included as much as what is there. What ideologies, whose voices, what epistemologies, and what knowledges are present or absent? These are just a few of the crucial questions to ask about curricula. An ecopedagogical example is when environmental disasters are taught, whose perspectives are in the teaching resources and not? Does the curriculum have, or allow space for, counterstories?

> **"Counterstories" defined**: Counterstorytelling as both a method of telling the story of those experiences that have not been told (i.e., those on the margins of society) and as a tool for analyzing and challenging the stories of those in power and whose story is a natural part of the dominant discourse the majoritarian story. ((Solorzano & Yosso, 2002) citing (Delgado, 1989))

These questions are not asked just to construct ecopedagogical curricula but also dialectic, problem-posing questions within ecopedagogical learning spaces. Ecopedagogues *and* students continuously ask whose silenced voices to bring into their learning space, with specific attention to including voices of those most socioenvironmentally oppressed. Also, problem-posing how best to get those voices into the ecopedagogical space is essential.

Epistemological Diversity and Limitations

What epistemologies is teaching being done through to counter, sustain, or intensify injustices and unsustainability must continuously be problematized. Previous discussions on teaching through the epistemologies of those in learning spaces must be included but also outside humanizing and planetarizing epistemologies are essential. In addition, problematizing epistemologies that justify environmental oppressions and domination of the rest of Nature is essential to disrupt them. Included in all this problematizing are the epistemological foundations of the disciplines and theories we teach and research through.

Santos (2018) utilized the scholarship of Bourdieu below to explain the need for rigorous self-reflexivity beyond one's own currently held epistemologies (of the North) that are often grounded in oppressions, hubris, and supremacy (e.g., "this" is the only correct way to think and know). He expressed the difficulties in such true reflexivity because the self's epistemologies are so very deep-seated in one's own identities and in "knowing" anything. I would align this with Freire's arguments of fear of conscientization.

> Bourdieu, a demanding exercise in self-reflexivity cannot but strengthen the belief in the monoculture of valid knowledge propounded by the epistemologies of the North. There is no room for bringing into account other ways of knowing that might correct or overcome the past failures of previous scientific knowledge or that might deal with other sets of issues. (Santos, 2018, p. 27)

Epistemologically limited reflexivity only strengthens previously held ways of knowing. Santos argues that self-reflection must include understanding that "the inquiry about limits is not an inquiry without limits" (Santos, 2018). Reflexivity in ecopedagogical dialogue and reading must be through "ecologies of knowledges" and limits of knowing. These limits include determining what is not known of the world-Earth (e.g., limits on knowing the Laws of Nature) and knowing others' world-Earth perceptions (i.e., "through others' eyes"). Teaching through ecologies of knowledges deepens and widens students' environmental understandings, but simultaneously problematizing cognitive limitations is also crucial.

Generative Themes

In the culture group Paulo Freire seeks to bring back the meaning of unity and synthesis between knowledge and life that had previously been gagged and smashed by the culture of capital, looking for generating themes in the universe of words of the community. These generating themes are "places" full of meanings of core experiences for existence that attach daily meanings to life. ... Since the generative theme speaks to people's experiences, it is generative, creative, because it dialogues with oppositions in an unstable balance. It contains significant values acquired through life experiences, which contaminate signs that express themselves and give birth to new persons. (Passos, 2012, p. 158)

Freirean education is problem-posing teaching through "generative themes," democratically determined by teacher(s) *and* students. Ecopedagogical teaching is through students' shared understandings of socioenvironmental issues—through "their 'generative themes' "—that are meaningful to them. As opposed to teaching through only educators' and administrators' understandings, students learn collectively through dialogue of theirs *with* others' realities of environmental violence.

Problem-posing method—dialogical par excellence—is constituted and organized by the students' view of the world, where their own generative themes are found. The content thus constantly expands and renews itself. The task of the dialogical teacher in an interdisciplinary team working on the thematic universe revealed by their investigation is to "re-present" that universe to the people from whom she or he first received it-and "re-present" it not as a lecture, but as a problem. (Freire, 2000, p. 109)

Robert Rhoads and Torres (2006) argued that "constructing generative themes builds an agenda for action to surmount 'limit situations.'" Problem-posing environmental violence through generative themes are acts of praxis to overcome barriers (i.e., limit situations) for achieving globally holistic socioenvironmental justice and planetary sustainability.

For example, if students are specifically concerned about their communities' actions to combat climate change, teachers would problem-pose what actions are needed, why, and the challenges to such actions (i.e., limit situations). These are only a sample of questions that would initiate dialogue on this generative theme. Rather than solely discussing the mechanics of climate change, dialogical teaching delves into the underlying reasons and politics of actions that continue to intensify global warming and possible ways to combat them.

Ecopedagogical problem-posing dialogue is not superficial. Such discussions should include the hidden politics of environmentally violent actions and associated complex conundrums. An example of a conundrum would be that the energy that gives us light, warmth, and powers our digital technologies is obtained from environmentally violent actions. Most likely, when the dialogue on environmentalism occurs, such energy sources are being used. This inherent conundrum poses a never-ending line of questioning about what is the baseline(s) of sustainability, as discussed previously, without causing others' de-_d_evelopment and environmental injustices, and within planetary sustainability guided by the Laws of Nature.

For a moment, let us put these conundrums aside and focus on teaching students to critically question the sources of energy we use (e.g., coal, solar, wind, hydro, nuclear) and why. If the answer is coal, problematizing why use coal rather than renewable sources? Within critical, Freirean terminology, what are the politics of those who most benefit from coal usage and who suffers, with the "who" including and beyond the anthroposphere? Answers not only lead to obvious aspects of coal companies benefiting financially but also how "we" might likely benefit too from coal's environmental violence that affects "them" and the rest of Nature. Socioenvironmental ills of the often marginalized coal-producing communities frequently result in "our" cheap prices for energy. Coal is just one example; nuclear energy and its hazards are others. Renewable energy has various questions, such as facility construction, limitations of location, and the mining for batteries' production. There are various vital aspects of Freirean teaching through generative themes; I will briefly unpack eight of them.

One: Commonalities

Every democratically constructed theme will not resonate highly with everyone in the space initially, especially within very diverse learning spaces. However, democratic decision-making through dialogue helps to determine socioenvironmental issues more significantly meaningful to students. Essential is the critical comparing of the commonalities between everyone's positionality(ies), understandings, and epistemological framings on the themes' socioenvironmental aspects, as much as the differences. Environmental pedagogies often fail by emphasizing us-versus-them differences of socioenvironmental violence—instilling a mystifying notion of "their" oppressions and an isolating uniqueness to "our" oppressions—rather than also including the commonalities between differing contexts (Misiaszek, 2011, 2012).

Freire (2000) argued that teaching through such binary divisions helps to "divide and conquer" the oppressed by weakening collective bottom-up resistance by avoiding teaching that oppressions occur across multiple, diverse populations. In other words, "I am"/"we are" the only ones environmentally oppressed in "this" way, and I/we do not have the power to fight against it. Environmental praxis is impossible through such teaching because of the entrenching fatalism of powerlessness. Themes might not initially seem important to some students until discussions begin that frequently link previously unknown and/or purposely hidden self-meaningfulness to them.

Two: Outside Ecopedagogical Spaces

Dialogue does not happen in vacuums, but other knowledges and ways of knowing are brought into learning spaces as learning resources, from books to media to outside lecturers, and much more. Ecopedagogical dialogue must include what understandings, voices, and epistemologies are not included within the learning space and what must be brought in. These inclusionary questions are also essential for ecopedagogical literacy to critically determine what is needed to be read next. In short, it is crucial to have endless critical questioning and re-questioning of "what is needed to know and how can we/I learn it?"

Three: Themes Connected to Lessons

Themes are connected to the learning objectives at hand. Generating themes is not open to any topic but rather coincide with the learning. This might seem intuitive, but I am often asked how students can learn without teachers giving their "expert" knowledge directly, and a free-for-all on topics selected by students does not occur. The foundational learning objectives remain, but the topics that teaching is *through* are democratically determined.

To illustrate this, I often give the example that if students in a mathematics course are interested in fast automobiles, we do not discuss automobiles in general. However, the art of critical teaching is constructing possibilities that the mechanics of automobiles and driving could be turned into mathematical learning (e.g., cylinders and fuel displacement with speed). Environmental teaching that I have argued as needed throughout all courses could take place in this example in dialogue on the unsustainability of excessively fast cars by questioning the mathematics of efficiency with cylinders, displacement, and speed. Or another example would be utilizing the mathematics of fuel consumption of gasoline versus electric vehicles (e.g., fossil fuel versus more single-source electric transportation). Math can also come into discussions on the conundrums of "environmentally friendly" modes of transportation and their battery disposal needs.

Four: Reflexivity and Unlearning

Teaching through generative themes also frequently calls for self "unlearning," including sometimes deep-seated ideologies. Freirean dialogue from problem-posing teaching is never free from conflict or limit situations; learning through dialogue is never easy but is demanding and requires rigorous teaching approaches. However, dialectical, problem-posing (environmental) teaching is essential for necessary transformation and praxis. Bohorquez (2008) argued that teaching must "pose obstacles to people becoming something more than they are—understanding these themes and wrestling with them is a step toward a fuller and more meaningful life" (Torres & Rhoads, 2005, p. 342).

Ideological disruption may include how we understand our world and the rest of Earth, how we see each other, what values we hold; the importance we place on individualism and collectivism; and how we measure success, development, and livelihood. These are just a few examples. Ecopedagogical work is through critical self-reflexivity, including contemplating the limitations of the self's reflexivity. Dialectic diversity of ecopedagogical teaching through generative themes is essential, as Rhodes and Torres (2006) describe below.

Refer to sets of issues that reflect themes within a particular epoch (particular point in time) and thematic universe of their epoch (subjectivity in reading the world) within which brings together a particular set of ideas, values, beliefs, hopes, doubts, and challenges.

Dialectic education means to "[call] forth a set of opposites of these issues in a dialectical fashion" (Rhoads & Torres, 2006), with conflict most likely emerging. This conflict emerges from our differing "set[s] of ideas, values, beliefs, hopes, doubts, and challenges." Rhoads and Torres' (2006) discussions on "epoch" indicate human unfinishedness and transformability, as opposed to teaching to seal a predestined, fixed fate for students.

Deepening and widening students' reflexivity within ecopedagogical spaces is "[re]locat[ing] the seat of their [(students')] decisions in themselves and in their relations with the world and others, people overcome the situations which limit them" (Freire, 2000). Ecopedagogical problem-posing must include how we locate ourselves in our environmental decision-making as it affects others and the rest of Nature? Who and what do we consider or not, well as to what depth? Ecopedagogical goals revolve around how we can further deepen and widen these understandings while also recognizing our limits of understanding.

Five: Limits of world-Earth Knowing

Self-reflexivity of what is not known and the limits of knowing the world-Earth is essential to problem-posing environmental violence in ecopedagogical spaces. People's and populations' differing histories and positionalities make understanding all of the world impossible. Absolute knowledge of all that makes up Earth is even less achievable. However, both should be utopic, though unreachable, learning goals. For example, if I spent every waking minute of my life studying environmental violence against girls in Afghanistan through ecofeminist lenses by reading every publication on the topic and spending years researching this population, it would not give me absolute knowledge on this topic. Nor would it mean that I would know the situation the same way as a girl living through the effects of environmental violence there. In addition, understanding environmental violence through non-anthropocentric perspectives brings in its own set of unique challenges.

People are complex with complex histories. However, teaching too often oversimplifies the reasons for individuals' or populations' (anti-)environmental actions, leading to othering them and a sense of hopelessness for justice and sustainability. Dialogue through generative themes must be critically reflexive of this vast diversity to conceptualize the limitations of knowing individuals and populations. Our knowledges are contextually fluid, shifting over time, as Freire expressed, in part, by his arguments on humans' innate unfinishedness. In addition, everyone has multiple identities, often coinciding and conflicting with one another in various ways. Teaching as though students are finished and can be summed up within a single identity is dehumanizing. Memmi (1967/1991) used the phrase "the mark the plural" for when colonizers placed a single identity upon an entire colonized population without exception or nuance—if you "know" one, then you "know" them all. Such taught ideologies dehumanize entire populations down to a single identity, only aiding to *other* members of a population.

Six: Laws of Nature Not Limit Situations

It is important to note that the Laws of Nature themselves are not limit situations when problem-posing environmental violence in classrooms. This is because limit situations are defined by Freire (2000) as obstacles to liberation. Nature outside of our world cannot oppress us because we, as humans who are part of Nature, live within Nature's Laws and limits, and does not cognitively cause violence to humans. Nature's Laws and limits are neither subjective nor flexible to our world's subjectivity.

For example, oppressions emerge from Earth having limited natural resources and the occurrence of natural disasters.

However, it is our constructed societal systems that lead to oppression. The extraction and distribution of natural resources and our building on sites where natural disasters frequently happen (e.g., building in earthquake-prone San Francisco and Tokyo) are examples. Another example that connects all this is our use of fossil fuels which contribute to global warming and, in turn, increase the frequency and intensity of natural disasters. To summarize, the non-anthropocentric sphere's mechanisms and resource limitations do not oppress us but are laws and limitations we must live within as part of Earth.

Seven: Utopias within Planetary Sustainability

Problematizing how our constructed utopias align and misalign with others' utopias for achieving worldwide social justice and sustainability beyond our world is essential. Ecopedagogies emphasize this latter part which is too often missing in (environmental) education. Problem-posing the gaps and limit situations between current environmental ills and an environmentally sustainable world need students and teachers to be able to dream of utopias leading to the latter. If we are fated to an environmentally unjust world and devastated Earth, problem-posing education is a fool's practice. This is what fatalism in education has us falsely believe and must be countered in ecopedagogies.

Ecopedagogical dialogue must include problematizing environmental violence from achieving humans' needs and wants associated with utopias that may oppress others and/or be planetarily unsustainable. For example, what should happen to homes in a forest when a fire naturally starts? Should the fire be put out even though burning the underbrush is essential for Nature's ways of fire management? These and similar questions are tough to answer. In teaching, (re)constructing generative themes around these and similar topics are complicated and almost guarantees some passionate dialogue, but are necessary as these need to be dealt with within realities.

Eight: Transdisciplinary

I have found that environmental teaching often occurs in artificial disciplinary vacuums, or silos, isolated from other disciplines (Misiaszek, 2011, 2012, 2015, 2018). Frequently this is not by mistake but systematically employed to artificially simplify socioenvironmental complexities that lead to environmental injustices and Nature's devastation. Numerous political reasons exist to suppress "radical" ecopedagogical praxis that challenges the current hegemony status quo. Environmental teaching in a single discipline makes it easier to isolate environmental violence to technocratic understandings and "deposit" false rationalities for them to occur.

> None of that can be offered by the technicist or mechanistically understood education. It is important to underscore, for well-intended but misguided educators, that the more education becomes empty of dreams to fight for, the more the emptiness left: by those dreams become with technique until the moment comes when education becomes reduced to that. Then, education becomes pure training, it becomes pure transfer of content, it is almost like the training of animals, it is a mere exercise in adaptation to the world. (Freire, 2004, p. 84)

Freire argued that learning and praxis are hindered by teaching siloed within a single discipline, segmenting understandings of the world-Earth that is anything but fragmented.

In other words, the world-Earth is limitlessly interconnected, but we often teach as though happenings occur in disciplinary vacuums. Such teaching hampers students' development and, thus, impedes *d*evelopment overall.

> Completely coherent with this vision is the concern for replacing the concept and practice that sees each part of the system as a separate entity. When each segment of the system

is isolated from the others, the learner's own development is forgotten and each stage becomes an alienating and alienated moment, merely a preparation for the next stage. (Freire, 1978, p. 42)

Mono-disciplinary teaching leads to students' dehumanizing adaption rather than any sense of participatory transformation of themselves and the world. Students are objectified in a segmented World that does not exist by removing the world's intersectionality and increasing world-Earth distancing. Curricula that disconnect and mystify students from the world-Earth holistically eradicate possibilities of ecopedagogical praxis. In turn, teaching becomes technically stepwise as becoming "merely a preparation for the next stage." This type of teaching leads to _D_evelopment for hegemonic others rather than for planetary sustainability and sustainable _d_evelopment.

An example of mono-disciplinary teaching's ill effects is the following. Teaching about coal mining only within the hard sciences fails to teach ecoracism issues of mining and histories of coloniality that have local coal towns worldwide not benefiting from (inter)national coal exports. Instead, these towns suffer from environmentally devastating outcomes locally (e.g., globalization as neocoloniality). Also, globally, twenty-five million to one billion people will be forced to migrate by 2050 (see International Organization for Migration (IOM, 2014)) due to global warming from, in part, burning coal. Technocratic environmental pedagogies have sciences, technology, engineering, and math (STEM) disciplines separated as though hard sciences' knowledges, practices, and research are not being influenced by politics, biases, and epistemological differences, among other influencing factors (Harding, 1991, 1998). The Laws of Nature are objective; however, humans' understandings and teaching of them are neither apolitical nor objective in the absolute sense. Ecopedagoigcal spaces inherently have transdisciplinary problem-posing of how STEM uses and understandings lead to either increased or decreased unsustainable environmental violence. This includes, but is not limited to, local-to-global problematizing of current aspects and uses of science held as "commonsense," histories of scientific work, and resulting _t_/_T_echnologies.

Freirean Pedagogy is NOT anti-environmental

Freire was talking about eco-pedagogy. In an interview at the Paulo Freire Institute, he talked of his love for the Earth, the animals, the plants: "I want to be remembered as somebody who loved the men, the women, the plants, the animals, the Earth," he said on that occasion. (Gadotti & Torres, 2009, pp. 1261–2)

Some scholars, including critical ones, have argued that Friere focused too much on socioeconomic class. Environmentalism is one of several important topics Freire has been criticized for not giving enough attention to in his work. Gender, race, and sexual orientation are other important topics argued as largely absent from his work. Wayne Au and Apple (2007) have pointed out that there are many worthy arguments on these absences, as any scholar's work can be critically deconstructed too. However, many of those arguing do so either by shallowly reading Freire's work or seem to think his work both began and ended with his writing of *Pedagogy of the Oppressed* (Freire, 2000; McLaren, 2007; Au & Apple, 2007; Misiaszek, 2011).

In the same way Freire discussed humans' innate unfinishedness, scholars are unfinished also, with their entire lifetime of work needing to be analyzed to fully understand their work. For example, during a lecture at Beijing Normal University, Apple pointed out that his work after writing *Ideology and Curriculum* (2004) was, and is, expansions and reinventions of this book to be taken as a work in progress rather than finished and fixed. Apple's argument should help us view Freire's work after *Pedagogy of the Oppressed* (2000).

Reading his later works is essential to understand Freire's environmentalism, especially *Pedagogy of Indignation* (2004), which was posthumously published and included some of his writings on ecopedagogy that were to become part of his next publication (Misiaszek & Torres, 2019).

There are several examples of critics reading his work shallowly. A key complaint is that Freire calls for endless transformation without cultural, epistemological, or historical contexts. They argue that such endless, non-contextual transformation disregards the local, as well as done without considering Nature's well-being and limits—or, in other words, lacking world-Earth sustainability considerations. In essence, they argue that Freirean problem-posing dialogue and conscientization within the learning space largely ignore all aspects outside of the space. However, these are misreadings of his work that, I would state with others (Freire, 2000; Au & Apple, 2007), is entirely opposite of what he advocated for.

Such critics misunderstand Freirean approaches as non-structured and undisciplined, relying solely on teaching from students' knowledge within physical learning spaces and thereby severely limiting what is taught. Some critics also argue that teachers dictate transformation within Freirean pedagogies but ignore Freire's arguments of democracy and authentic dialogue in learning spaces that he further ironed out throughout his lifetime of work. Dialectical education is not only discussions within ecopedagogical spaces but also what is outside the spaces. Ecopedagogues bring in voices through various means. In short, voices within ecopedagogical spaces are important, but it is also essential to bring in outside, diverse voices to be critically read and discussed through the students' and teachers' understandings and epistemologies within the spaces. It is crucial to determine what voices and epistemologies are absent to truly understand oppressions to, in turn, bring those voices meaningfully into learning spaces (Santos, 2018; Apple, 2004; Gadotti, 1996). This is also needed for ecopedagogical research to determine whose voices (i.e., participants) will be heard or not, which methodologies will be used or not, and what epistemological lenses will be utilized or not. In addition, self-reflexivity within ecopedagogical reading is accomplished by continuously problematizing these and similar critical questions.

I want to dismiss one last criticism: Freire's comparing humans' unfinishedness and transformability to other Earth's beings is not anti-environmental.

> Awareness of the world, which makes awareness of myself viable, makes unviable the immutability of the world. Awareness of the world and awareness of myself make me not only a being in the world, but one with the world and *with* others. It makes me a being capable of intervening in the world and not only of adapting to it. It is in this sense that women and men can interfere in the world while other animals can only touch it. That is why not only do we have a history, but we make our history, which equally makes us, and thus makes us historic. (Freire, 2004, p. 15)

Freire is neither devaluing animals nor saying that animals do not have means of communication, but "human activity is theory and practice; it is reflection and action [i]t cannot be reduced to either verbalism or activism" (Freire, 2000). His quotes emphasize that only humans can develop through positive or negative transformation, while animals adapt and evolve by reacting to their immediate and current surroundings. Freire's use of the word "intervening" above indicates acts that define us as being human. Intervention to disrupt socioenvironmental injustices and unsustainability beyond anthropocentrism is included, as these are the praxis goal of ecopedagogies. Overall, only humans can have reflexive dialogue that leads to praxis. I read and reinvent his words as calling upon humans' socioenvironmental responsibility as beings as part of the world-Earth, as opposed to others who have misread his words as anti-environmental.

An example of Freire (2004) discussing human uniqueness is his utilization of Marx comparing bees to architects below.

At a certain point in Capital, while discussing human work as opposed to that of other animals, Marx says that a bee could not possibly compare to even the most "modest" of architects. After all, a human being has the capacity for ideating an object before ever producing it. The carpenter has the table drawn up in his or her head before building it. This inventive capacity implies a communicative one, on all levels of the vital experience. The creative and communicative activities of human beings, however, connote qualities that are exclusively their own. Communication exists in life, but human communication is processed as well, all especially so, in existence, a human invention. (Freire, 2004, p. 120)

Freire here is not belittling bees' capabilities, work, or value but rather is differentiating humans' ability to reflexively invent and reinvent our World within Earth, for the good and bad. In fact, bees are one of the most needed beings on Earth as they pollinate plants and flowers, resulting in food, oxygen, and many other necessary aspects of the world-Earth. Unfortunately, global warming is currently causing a massive reduction of bees worldwide. Freire's call for humans to be stewards of Nature can be read through his later work, some of which are given as quotes throughout this book. He argued that respecting and loving the rest of Nature grounds his pedagogy.

CHAPTER FOUR

Ecopedagogical Praxis from Theories

Human activity consists of action and reflection: it is praxis; it is transformation of the world. And as praxis, it requires theory to illuminate it. Human activity is theory and practice; it is reflection and action. It cannot ... be reduced to either verbalism or activism.
(Freire, 2000, p. 125)

Praxis has many definitions and framings. Below, Gadotti (1996) defined praxis as actions through dialogue and theories to begin his book *Pedagogy of Praxis: A Dialectical Philosophy of Education*.

> The notion of "praxis" in traditional Western philosophy is more analytically complex than is the notion of practice or conflict per se. Indeed it is more appealing for those who would like to consider the relationships between theory and practice as blended together in the notion of praxis, a dialectical concept. (Gadotti, 1996, p. xvi)

Ecopedagogical praxis, which has been discussed already to some extent, is grounded in ending unsustainable environmental violence. This does not mean critical, Freirean pedagogies are absent from this goal, but rather this overall grounding differentiates ecopedagogies from other pedagogies. For example, ecopedagogues strive to disrupt unsustainable _D_evelopment through praxis.

Me uttering the term "theory," including saying any "isms," often terrifies my students, as it did me as a student initially. Too often, theories are mystified and are forced upon students without explaining why we use them, their sociohistorical roots, and/or their importance. Students frequently say they dislike theories because they like "real-world practice."

> Critical reflection on your praxis is absolutely indispensable. It should never be confused with meaningless alienating and alienated talk. While it is the source of knowledge, praxis is not, however, a theory in itself. It is only when we give ourselves constantly to critical reflection on it that praxis makes possible the development of theory, which, in its turn, illumines new practice. (Freire, 1978, p. 125)

I frequently begin my courses by asking what theories and theoretical frameworks are and why do we use them. Freire argued that good theories emerge from the "real world," as his scholarship did (Schugurensky, 2011; Torres, 2014).

Theories emerge from human activities and praxis "requires theory to illuminate it ... [h]uman activity is theory and practice; it is reflection and action" (Freire, 2000). Praxis is hegemony's enemy, including unjust power from environmental violence, because students' reflexivity is likely to lead to challenging ideologies that sustain dominance. Marx argued that the best way to dominate someone is not by direct force but by ideologically hiding the domination itself. Even more effective is having the oppressed falsely believe that what oppresses them benefits them. An obvious current example is Trump's US election win in 2016 from his strongest supporters, who are most likely to be the most significantly hurt by his neoliberal, anti-environmental policies. The overall goal of using theories in ecopedagogical spaces is to unveil and better understand oppressions and unsustainability and the local-to-global politics of why they occur.

Banking (environmental) education, at best, does not challenge such false ideologies and, at worst, further entrenches them. Banking pedagogies are necessary tools for domination and unsustainability (Gadotti, 1996; Giroux, 2001; Gadotti & Torres, 2009). Banking approaches systematically deny praxis to counter taught oppressive, unsustainable ideologies in the classroom and do not provide students the tools to counter them outside the classroom. Theories used in banking spaces have these same characteristics, with goals opposite to the one I have discussed for critical, ecopedagogical spaces.

I argue, with Freire and others, that theories must be demystified in environmental teaching. I am not arguing for simplifying or narrowing theories in ecopedagogies to, in turn, simplify and narrow understandings of the world-Earth, but quite the opposite—to being meaningful and contextual "lenses" for better understanding the world-Earth's complexities and messiness (Misiaszek, 2021). This metaphor of theories as lenses emerges from the work of Torres and other critical scholars.

"Good" use of theoretical lenses allows us to deepen and widen our understandings of others and others' perspectives of socioenvironmental violence to determine our praxis. Thus, ecopedagogical usage of "good" theories is for praxis toward ending socioenvironmental oppressions and planetary unsustainability rather than just knowing about them without taking action (Misiaszek & Torres, 2019). Freire (2000) expressed that:

> Action is human only when it is not merely an occupation but also a preoccupation, that is, when it is not dichotomized from reflection (Freire 2004, p. 53); ... discovery cannot be purely intellectual but must involve action; nor can

it be limited to mere activism, but must include serious reflexivity—only then will it be a praxis." (p. 65)

Without goals of praxis, education is not critical (Gadotti, 1996), nor ecopedagogical, and the use of theories is in vain. Theories without leading to praxis-based goals are virtually meaningless and useless for essential environmental transformation. The selection of theories within ecopedagogical spaces is guided by goals of overcoming limit situations that bar us from ending socioenvironmental injustices and unsustainability. Theories should help to more deeply understand oppressions from the eyes of the oppressed by environmental violence.

Using my previous example of Afghanistan girls, we must ask how can we use theories of feminism, ecofeminism, globalizations, and coloniality, among others, to understand their oppressions better.. In other words, how can we use theories to better read the limitations of our understandings and self-reflexivity? For example, as a heterosexual, white, Western male, what are my limitations in understanding others' oppression worldwide? Queer theories, critical race theories, feminist theories, and theories of (neo)coloniality, to name a few, can often help me better to understand oppressions and the limits of my understandings.

As well, theoretical lenses should help us widen our understandings of the local-to-global politics of environmental violence and the effects of the violence for all of Earth, including beyond humans and beyond anthropocentric concerns.

Reinventing Theories

Reinvention is essential in ecopedagogies, as in all Freirean pedagogies—"for historicization and nondogmatic reinvention" (Morrow, 2019; Freire, 1985, 1992, 1993, 1996, 2004). Because the world is unfinished, theories need continuous reinvention. Critical reflexivity is using theories to demystify the world-Earth, "illumin[ing] new practice[s]" (Freire, 1978) for effective praxis to occur. Reinventing theories must emerge from their essence. For example, reinventing Freire's work can neither lead to apoliticizing or deradicalizing his essence, nor remove his work's goals of social justice—a far too-frequent occurrence (Au & Apple, 2007). Reinventing theories within ecopedagogical work are rooted in goals to end unsustainable environmental violence; any reinventions without this rooted goal are perverted uses in ecopedagogies.

Local reinventions of theories can lead to authentic praxis; without local contextualization, theories cannot determine viable solutions to the problems at hand (Gadotti, 1996). Freire's argument for needing to reinvent pedagogies and theories continuously included his own. He told people not to blindly follow him but rather reinvent his work to be contextually meaningful. He emphasized the need for bottom-up reinvention. Freire would sometimes be asked for solutions to local problems, to which he would answer that he does not know because he does not know the local contexts well. He would say that he could listen and give insights on what worked or not in other locations. He emphasized that solutions emerge through bottom-up decision-making and actions.

Disrupting Fear

Ecopedagogical praxis is neither simple nor easy, even when leading to one's own liberation. Praxis often includes disrupting people's deep-seated ideologies, which are often viewed as commonsense and form their self-identities and positionalities (Torres, 2011; Santos, 2018). Freire wrote about how challenging it is to challenge one's own ingrained ideologies even when the ideologies form oppressions onto the self. Or, when ideologies provide privileges to the self—this will be discussed later through Freire's notions of the difficulties in *class suicide*. For example, challenging _D_evelopment and associated terms in ecopedagogical spaces can be difficult because it radically disrupts many years of taught ideologies of world order. Also, thinking about _d/D_evelopment within widened lenses can seem very foreign. This all contributes to students' and teachers' fears of liberation. Freire (1998, 2000) discussed the overcoming of fear in challenging notions perceived as unquestionable, disrupting notions normalized as being "natural" even though they lead to oppressions, dominance, and unsustainability. Teaching for ecopedagogical praxis to overcome such fear and disrupting the dogma of such ideological framings *is* ecopedagogical work.

Countering the self's oppressions as "normal" is necessary but difficult and requires courage to overcome fear.

> [Humans] become domesticated by the new contents which the leaders deposit in them. In other circumstances, they may become frightened by a "word" which threatens the oppressor housed within them. (Freire, 2000, p. 135)

Freire's phrase "oppressor housed within them" does not indicate pragmatic domination but rather how the oppressed see themselves through the oppressors' eyes—in other words—internalizing their subaltern-*ness*. Oppressed:oppressor is not binary, nor dualistic, with a group as oppressed and another group who are the oppressors (see Torres, 2015). Instead, everyone is *both* an oppressor *and* is oppressed. Disrupting domestication needs continuous problem-posing of how ideologies justify socioenvironmental oppressions and planetary unsustainability. Domesticating the oppressed in (environmental) education is through systematically silencing discussions of "uncomfortable" thoughts that disrupt oppressive/domineering but normalized ideologies (Misiaszek & Torres, 2019). Overcoming fears of liberation and unsustainability is by critically questioning the often "unquestionable"—foundational aspects of ecopedagogies.

Radical, Collective Praxis

Ecopedagogical praxis is innately radical because emergent actions aim to end hegemonic systems and structures that enable unsustainable environmental violence. Whenever hegemony is challenged, including in education, it is labeled as "radical." This label is taught as inherently harmful, even though the opposite is frequently true. "Radical" teaching is opposite to top-down banking teaching that is absent of possible transformable actions because unveiling and challenging dominant politics of environmental violence are nonexistent.

Ecopedagogical praxis is naturally collective. In his last chapter of *Pedagogy of the Oppressed* (2000), Freire discussed how revolutionary leaders and organizations need to be "in communion [to] liberate each other," as further expressed below.

> Legitimately say that in the process of oppression someone oppresses someone else; we cannot say that in the process of revolution someone liberates someone else, nor yet that someone liberates himself, but rather that human beings in communion liberate each other. (p. 133)

> The oppressed and the leaders are equally the Subjects of revolutionary action, and reality serves as the medium for the transforming action of both groups. In this theory of action one cannot speak of an actor, nor simply of actors, but rather of actors in intercommunication. (p. 129)

Praxis emerges from collective dialectics to understand each other's realities. Praxis cannot emerge if persons' realities are silenced as banking educators attempt to do within *their* teaching spaces (emphasizing "their" because banking spaces are not shared with students).

"Radical" environmental pedagogies and emergent praxis have increasingly been on the defense as environmental injustices and unsustainability have been further entrenched by a majority of environmental teaching as "natural," insignificant, or just not occurring. Santos (2018) below expressed this as an unfortunate global phenomenon.

> Most morally repugnant forms of social inequality and social discrimination are becoming politically acceptable. The social and political forces that used to challenge this state of affairs in the name of possible social and political alternatives seem to be losing steam and, in general, appear to be everywhere on the defensive. (Santos, 2018, p. vii)

Teaching for an undeniable fate of injustice and unsustainability is an effective way to extinguish protest on hegemony built upon environmental violence. Thus, disrupting fatalistic education that teaches for a singular oppressive future rather than possibilities of plural futures is radical in itself. Teaching that environmental transformation is possible is a critical first step in educating for ecopedagogical praxis.

Globalization from Above and Anthropocentrism

Local environmental degradation and injustices do not occur in apolitical vacuums without outside influences; however, many banking educators teach that they do. As previously argued, globalization is a contested terrain. Processes of globalization (i.e., globalizations) both help and hinder the necessary global collectivity for planetary sustainability. Intensifying globalization has furthered the need to be an active member of one's local society(ies), an active member of the world (e.g., a global citizen), and act as being *part of* Earth/Nature holistically (e.g., a planetary citizen).

Ecopedagogical praxis includes determining how globalizations from above can be countered and, in turn, strengthen globalization processes from below. Environmental ills, especially those near their "tipping points," require globally-holistic solutions with worldwide impact. For example, praxis to solve global warming cannot happen only in a few select regions without global-wide actions. Limiting fossil fuel usage only in the Global South will not end rising ocean levels without the same happening in the North. In this example, ecopedagogical praxis should emerge from better global understandings of why fossil fuels are being used so prevalently as energy sources. Included are aspects such as intensifying hegemony of the Global North from histories of colonization. Thus, intensifying globalization is neocoloniality in many aspects. What also needs problematizing is how to utilize global processes from below to disrupt such neocoloniality.

Widened planetary lenses beyond global ones are essential to problematize questions such as the following. How does education affect the valuing of Nature outside of humans? What taught epistemologies and belief systems center humans in ways that all else of Earth is devalued? How does such devaluing result in world-Earth distancing, which, in turn, forms our epistemological framings of "development" and "progress?" Our human abilities to critically problematize these and similar questions place Nature's sustainability holistically upon our shoulders and responsibility for Nature's demise if left unproblematized. Ecopedagogues must radically disrupt Illich's (1983) characteristics of "contemporary man" (i.e., "us" as humans in modern society), who are mostly taught to avoid such questioning.

CHAPTER FIVE

Development for Justice and Sustainability

*Education is itself a dimension of social practice.
It seeks to know the reason for the practice and,
through this knowledge as it deepens and develops,
it also seeks new practice that is consistent with the
overall plan for the society. (Freire, 1978, p. 89)*

As Freire hints above, there are conflictual roles of education as being influenced by contested terrains of *d/D*evelopment, as well as a tool for development (i.e., "overall plan for the society"). Throughout the previous chapters, teaching for development has been problematized by asking how we are taught the measurements and goals of "progress," "growth," "modernization," and "success." among other terms associated with development. Problematized differently, how are we taught to understand these terms' antagonyms: regression, de-growth, being traditional, and failure? Teaching through dialectically deconstructing development is essential for praxis from ecopedagogical conscientization that has students actively disrupting *D*evelopment and learning development simply as _d_evelopment. Teaching ecopedagogical literacy aids in accomplishing this.

Education for sustainable development (ESD) largely emerged from environmental education (EE) models to, in part, re-focus anti-environmentalism as affecting societies to, in turn, (re-)frame "development" as not to impede on our and others' wellbeing in the future, including future generations' wellbeing, by destroying _n_/_N_ature ("n/N" letter casing is dependent on ESD model). In other words, teaching how we can progress without oppressing ourselves and others in the future is crucial, as well as not destroying the environment. EE was largely viewed as conservation-based pedagogies that did not deal with issues that plagued societies. For example, urban environmental issues and ecoracism are often absent from mainstream EE curricula in the US. Unfortunately, ESD models have been increasingly guided by _D_evelopment ideologies that lack local-contextual aspects of what is needed and wanted socially and environmentally. I designate these models as ESD (education for sustainable _D_evelopment) as opposed to ESd (education for sustainable _d_evelopment). In Freirean approaches, ecopedagogues critically question "What is?," "For whom?," and "Who defines?" development and associated sustainability. The ecopedagogical goal is countering _D_evelopment without regard for planetary sustainability.

_d_evelopment is not shifting the spoils of _D_evelopment from the oppressors to the oppressed, nor shifting the resulting hegemony. Rather, the goal is praxis for globally holistic _d_evelopment and global absence of hegemony. Ecopedagogies align with Freire's (2000) calls to disrupt "success" characterized by increasing the number of people "beneath" the self. Gadotti (1996), through Freire's work, pointed out the unfortunate aspect that when the oppressed "succeed" under such measurements, they frequently become worse oppressors than their (previous) oppressors.

I have argued in my previous work, along with other educational scholars, that public education emerged for two overall tasks: teaching for development and teaching for citizenship. This chapter will further unpack how ecopedagogical work is for _d_evelopment leading to local-to-global environmental justice and local-to-planetary sustainability. As I have already argued, this also means teaching to counter _D_evelopment. The next chapter will focus on the contested terrain of education for citizenships (within and between local-to-planetary citizenship spheres).

Livelihood

> Structural changes in the society depend on many factors. ... There is a dialectical relationship—unity and the opposition of contraries—between structure and consciousness. ... At the PFI [Paulo Freire Institute], we insist on linking the individual dimension of consciousness with the social and collective dimension of organizational work. For instance, it is not enough to change your individual lifestyle to make the world more sustainable. It is necessary to change the system that produces an unsustainable lifestyle; one that produces injustices and inequalities simultaneously. (Antunes et al., 2019, p. 578)

Ecopedagogical dialogue and reading on how individual lifestyle choices are connected to sustainable environmental violence are essential to understanding local-to-planetary consequences better. Such reflexivity includes recognizing that the term "lifestyle" and determining one's own "lifestyle" is a privilege because much of the world struggles to merely survive. I have heard many times that the Global North has "lifestyles" while the Global South has skills for existing due to Northern lifestyles. These are the reasons why I use the term "livelihood" in my work instead of "lifestyle."

Freire (2000) argued that class suicide is nearly impossible in which a person gives up all their power and privileges. This unlikelihood is increasing with intensifying neoliberal globalizations penetrating almost every corner of the world.

Neoliberalism instills an ideology that privileges should not be problematized but should be strived to obtain. Critically questioning "who" is socioenvironmentally oppressed in the name of others' livelihood is frequently absent from environmental pedagogies. Non-anthropocentric questioning of our roles in Nature's devastation to increase livelihood is much more absent.

When those benefiting from _D_evelopment vocally oppose their livelihood to be negatively affected by sustainable _d_evelopment approaches, ecopedagogical teaching problem-poses how their _D_evelopment leads to others' de-_d_evelopment and the reasons why we should care. There are also ecopedagogical goals of understanding and caring beyond anthropocentric concerns of humans' wants and sometimes human needs.

Freire's (2000) arguments of committing one's own class suicide as nearly impossible begs the following question: Who is willing to give up their privileges from _D_evelopment? A more specific, poignant question to ask when people are hesitant to give up their lifestyle or a certain level of livelihood is the following: Would "they" be willing to give up what they ask others to forgo? Freire answers this question below.

> They demand of the rest of the world now what they were unwilling to demand of themselves. One of the tricks of their fatalistic ideology is the capacity to convince submissive economies (which will be engulfed in this process) that the real world is this way, that there is nothing to be done about it except to follow the natural order of the facts. It passes off this ideology as natural or almost natural. It does not want us to see and understand the phenomenon as a product of historical development. (Freire, 1998, p. 114)

This question becomes complicated for numerous reasons, including when privileges are taught as justified, such as through ideologies of Western exceptionalism, White supremacy, coloniality, patriarchy, and humans as the center of the universe. Histories of these and other oppressions are the histories Freire, in part, is referring to that are purposely absent from education, including education for _D_evelopment. These are, without a doubt, limit situations of environmental pedagogies leading to necessary transformative praxis for _d_evelopment. I would argue that challenging the impossibleness of class suicide is to disrupt them by problematizing positionalities of privilege, including the self's. Current and aspirational livelihoods must be ecopedagogically discussed and read within globally inclusive justice and local-to-planetary sustainability. Such problematizing is even more important when the term "lifestyle" is invoked. Increasing one's livelihood does not necessarily mean lowering others' livelihoods, and unsustainable environmental violence will ensue, but neoliberal gains in livelihood will undoubtedly have these results.

Authentic _d_evelopment

Banking education systematically suppresses reflexivity crucial for _d_evelopment and is essential for alienating _D_evelopment that is normalized as development overall. Freire (2000) expressed this below.

> Men who are submitted to concrete conditions of oppression in which they become alienated "beings for another" of the false "being for himself" on whom they depend, are not able to develop authentically. Deprived of their own power of decision, which is located in the oppressor, they follow the prescriptions of the latter. The oppressed only begin to develop when, surmounting the contradiction in which they are caught, they become "beings for themselves." (Freire, 2000, p. 161)

Education for _D_evelopment does not lead to students becoming "beings for themselves" or for _their d_evelopment (i.e., authentic development), but rather beings for others and _others' D_evelopment. Teaching for this conscientization is paramount in ecopedagogies. Utilizing Hegelian terms within ecopedagogical framings, students become the slaves for maters' _D_evelopment. Liberation and planetary sustainability are only able to come about once students recognize they are the hosts of others' _D_evelopment and, in turn, their own de-_d_evelopment.

Teaching to disrupt labor for _D_evelopment rather than authentic _d_evelopment is ecopedagogical work. Problematizing what _is_ "labor" and "production" for _d_/_D_evelopment is essential to unveil and counter ES_D_ for advancing ES_d_.

> If production is governed by the wellbeing of the total society, rather than by the capitalist, private or state, then the accumulation of capital-indispensable to development-has a totally different significance and goal. The part of the accumulated capital that is not paid to the worker is not taken from him but is his quota toward the development of the collectivity. And what is to be produced with this quota are not goods defined as necessarily salable but good that are socially necessary. For this it is essential that a society reconstruct itself in a revolutionary manner if it intends to become a society of workers whose leadership renounces both the tendency to leave everything to chance and the hardening of bureaucracy. (Freire, 1978, p. 105)

Freire's passage above introduces aspects of collective labor as development and livelihood. I would argue that the aspects of collectivity align with necessary renouncing and actively unlearning _D_evelopment ideologies and, what will be argued in the next chapter, necessary citizenships education for local-to-planetary collectivity.

_Radical Hope for _d_evelopment_

As discussed previously, there are various crucial intersecting aspects of utopia and education for transformable praxis for _d_evelopment. Socioenvironmental transformation cannot occur without hope—seeing ourselves, others, our world overall, and Earth's unsustainability as finished. As such, environmental hope is seen as leading nowhere, untethering injustices and unsustainability guided by _D_evelopment. Adapting to finished systems of _D_evelopment is a dehumanizing _change_ as opposed to development or transformation. Banking (environmental) pedagogical models domesticate us to these falsely finished systems.

_D_evelopment's success is primarily due to taught fatalism; teaching for radical hope is essential for _d_evelopment. Aspects of "radicalness" are essential because _D_evelopment is being widely taught as a finished, foundational ideology to guide our thoughts and decision-making.

> Domination is itself objectively divisive. It maintains the oppressed in a position of "adhesion" to a reality which seems all powerful and overwhelming, and then alienates by presenting mysterious forces to explain this power. (Freire, 2000, p. 173)

Simply put, without teaching for hope of bettering the world, education blindly adheres students to socioenvironmentally oppressive realities and a singular future of _D_evelopment.

Education must be grounded in the "faith in humankind" (Freire, 2000), teaching "through conscientization [in which] subjects assume their historical commitment in the process of making and remaking the world, within concrete possibilities, also making and remaking themselves" (Freitas, 2012).

> If it is possible to reach water by digging up the ground, if it is possible to decorate a house, if it is possible to believe this or that truth, if it is possible to find shelter from cold and heat, if it is possible to alter the course of rivers and to build dams, if it is possible to change the world we have not created, that of nature, why not change the world of our own creation, that of culture, of history, of politics? (Freire, 2004, p. 82)

Freire asks the following relatively simple question: if we can physically transform the environment, which could be for _d_evelopment or _D_evelopment, why are students taught that transforming our world constructed by our histories is impossible? Ecopedagogues teach on the transformability of our world's unfinishedness to disrupt oppressions, domination, and devastation emergent from our "created" social systems and physical changes to Nature done in the name of _D_evelopment.

Decolonizing Development

(Neo)coloniality inherently objectifies the (neo)colonized so that their authentic _d_evelopment is impossible (Memmi, 1967/1991; Said, 1979; Fanon, 1963). As emphasized previously, Freire's argued that everyone needs to be taught as Subjects rather than objects. Freire's words below express how coloniality denied the colonized of their histories and cultures; this is also denying them of histories _and_ futures of _d_evelopment.

> Only the colonizers "have a history," since the history of the colonized is presumed to have begun with the civilizing presence of the colonizers. Only the colonizers "have" culture, art and language and are civilized national citizens of the world which "saves" others. The colonized lacked a history before the "blessed" efforts of the colonizers. The colonized are uncultured and "barbarian natives." (Freire, 1978, p. 126)

Colonized _D_evelopment is founded upon dominant, Northern histories, cultures, and epistemologies. Southern _d_evelopment is falsely taught as absurd through globalizations akin to neocoloniality for _D_evelopment. Ecopedagogues teach to critically recognize and disrupt _D_evelopments' coloniality. Such teaching is not only essential for the (neo)colonized themselves but for _d_evelopment worldwide. I often pose to students the question, what development has the world lost by the North systematically oppressing most of the world?

Through Freirean lenses, Gadotti and Torres (2009) argued that banking education and histories of colonialization in Brazil, for example, have severely thinned democracy and have blocked Brazilians' *authentic development* (termed _d_evelopment in my work). They argue that a "cultural backwardness," or I would add "developmental backwardness," has unfortunately emerged from banking teaching that does neither lead to populations' development nor thick democracy, but rather _D_evelopment for their (neo)colonizers (Gadotti & Torres, 2009). They call for ecopedagogical teaching in Brazil to critically reinvent development that is actually *for* Brazil's masses, as well as for environmental sustainability through arguments of local-to-planetary citizenships education. These needs coincide with Gadotti's (2008b, 2008a, 1996) other writings on Gaia and planetary citizenship education and Torres's (2017a, 2017b; Tarozzi & Torres, 2013, 2016) writings on multicultural education and critical GCE.

Sciences and Technologies

In his introduction to Freire's *Pedagogy of Freedom* (1998) book, Stanley Aronowitz (1998) emphasizes, through Freire's arguments of our innate unfinishedness, that framings of being pedagogically "scientific" can be a tool to instill false finishedness.

> Freire stands firmly in the tradition for which the definition of science is critical and not positivistic. Educational formation becomes "scientific" when the learner grasps the link between theory arid practice through a process whose assumption is that the individual is, in every respect, "unfinished." The accomplishment of critical consciousness consists in the first place in the learner's capacity to situate herself in her own historicity, for example, to grasp the

class, race, and sexual aspects of education and social formation and to understand the complexity of the relations that have produced this situation. Such an accomplishment entails a critical examination of received wisdom, not as a storehouse of eternal truths but as itself situated in its own historicity. Implicit in this process is the concept that each of us embodies universality but that it does not necessarily dominate us. Thus, the active knower, not the mind as a repository of "information," is the goal of education. (Aronowitz, 1998, p. 14)

Teaching students to become "active knower[s]" who ecopedagogically read sciences as political, non-static, and truth-seeking or not is an important goal for ecopedagogues. This last characteristic of truth-seeking is essential to differentiate critical problem-posing sciences as opposed to political opinions that create and emerge from post-truths. For example, knowledges' fluidity and subjectivity do not legitimize climate change denial. Knowledges, sciences, and technologies that lead to _D_evelopment must be endlessly problematized for future_s_ of _d_evelopment.

Freire did not diminish the need for science education but rather the need for sciences to be humanizing and, in his later work specifically, planetarizing. Problematizing (de-) humanizing aspects of _s/S_ciences, its teachings, and _s/S_cientific research ask how "science" benefit some and not others, and why. (De-)planetarizing questions center around how _s/S_cience helps or hinders planetary sustainability. Are these differences due to objectivity, which is often touted as "being scientific" work, or from subjectivity and politics? It is important here to emphasize again that Freire saw apolitical, objective sciences as impossible.

The essential content in any educational program-whether on syntax, biology, physics, mathematics, or the social sciences—is that which makes possible discussions of the mutable Nature of natural reality, as well as of history, and which sees men and women as beings capable, not only of adapting to the world but above all of changing in it. It must view men and women as curious, engaged, talkative, creative beings. (Freire, 2004, p. 79)

Ecopedagogical work questions the epistemological manipulation of _s/S_cientific knowledges that leads toward _D_evelopment and, in turn, de-_d_evelopment. For example, (neo-)colonizers have inserted their _S_ciences and _K_nowledges for oppressive control, including manipulating the (neo) colonialized's _s_ciences, _k_nowledges, and _t_echnologies for their profiteering (Harding, 1991, 1998, 2006).

Problematizing the (de-)planetarizing*ness* of sciences and its emergent technologies widens the deconstructing of sciences' positive and negative aspects affecting us to include the rest of Nature in the term "us." This questioning includes which _s/S_ciences epistemologically consider humans as part of Nature and which ones do not. In addition, how sciences include or exclude us epistemologically and ecolinguistically from the non-anthroposphere. The fundamental ecopedagogical question here is what local-to-global-to-planetary spheres are considered when determining legitimate goals and methodologies. For example, what and "who" is considered with _S_ciences and research leading to natural resource mining or forest destruction for "efficient" corporate _F_arming (Epstein-HaLevi et al., 2018) or weapon technologies. Beyond socioenvironmental injustices caused by these technologies, which may or may not be considered, will environmental devastation be non-anthropocentrically considered in _S_ciences? These are some crucial reasons for needing to utilize a diversity of _s/S_ciences—Indigenous, Eastern, Southern, Northern, Western, and other sciences.

Technologies labeled as "advancements" must be critically deconstructed on _who_ will "benefit" and _who_ will "suffer" from their usage, with the _who_, again, expanded planetarily. An example is questioning the initial conceptualized and actual "endpoints" or "goals" of technologies. Are Facebook's initial goals to connect people to the same endpoints that manipulated, through their algorithms to keep users scrolling down, a US presidential election in 2016? Or helped intensify the COVID-19 pandemic by widely spreading misinformation?

Parallel with _s_ciences, Freire stressed that technologies (specifically _t_echnologies) should be "produc[ing] a tomorrow" (2004) that is a better world, rather than reproducing the world's oppressions. Below, he problematizes a globalized "tomorrow" blindly guided technologies and economies.

> The globalization of the economy or technological advances, for example, are not in themselves defining of a tomorrow given as certain, a sort of improved extension of a certain expression of today. Globalization does not put an end to politics, rather, it creates the need to engage in the latter differently. While globalization may tend to weaken the effectiveness of strikes in the struggle of workers, it does not mean the end of the fight. (Freire, 2004, p. 75)

Freire's overall question is more relevant today than when he wrote it many years ago. How have globalizations been guided by, and resulted in, _T_echnologies that reproduced oppressions and entrenched fatalism? I would include planetary unsustainability to this question and ask what are the possibilities of _t_echnologies that can emerge from globalizations from below. Reinventing Freire's work, ecopedagogues incorporate non-anthropocentric lenses to such problematizing of globalizations and _t/T_echnologies.

Freire's previous quote I gave on blindly adopting neoliberalism as similar to jumping on a train without knowing its destination (1998), coincides with blindly following, creating, and using technologies as unquestionable "advancements" for development. Kahn (2010) has argued that ecopedagogues must determine the possibilities of radically shifting usages of technologies as tools of violence, oppressions, and unsustainability for ecopedagogical "re-tooling."

Retooling the internet is an obvious example. The internet increases access to information but also limits real, full access through, for example, search engine and social media algorithms. Censorship and the digital divides also limit access to knowledges online. The internet has essential truth-seeking information but also fuels post-truths that justify unsustainable socioenvironmental violence. Critically questioning if being online diversifies what we "know" or whether it solidifies previously held knowledges and epistemologies that reproduce oppressions and planetary unsustainability is endless in ecopedagogical work. Kahn (2010) argues that ecopedagogues must teach to transform the internet and its usage for the former and counter the latter. Part of retooling the internet is teaching that helps deepen and widen meaningful interconnectedness while not devaluing the world's diversity or the rest of Nature's well-being. This work is also done in post-digitalism and ecopedagogy (Jandrić & Ford, 2022; Misiaszek et al., 2022, see Jandrić & Ford, 2020).

Problematizing sciences and technologies calls for:

A type of curiosity that can defend us from the excess of a rationality that now inundates our highly technologized world. Which does not mean that we are to adopt a false humanist posture of denying the value of technology and science. On the contrary, it's a posture of balance that neither deifies nor demonizes technology. A posture that is from those who consider technology from a critically curious standpoint. (Freire, 1998, p. 38)

Teaching students to view sciences and technologies as apolitical, ahistorical, acontextual, and overall unproblematic, is the opposite of what Freire argues. Ecopedagogues teach to disrupt the manipulation, isolation, and apoliticization of sciences and technologies through diverse epistemologies, knowledges, contexts, and disciplines (including disciplines with diverse epistemological foundations). Ecopedagogical teaching has students understand the world-Earth through "a posture of balance" and always have "critically curious standpoint(s)." Technologies, such as the internet, can help with this, but can also hinder such education.

Bottom-Up Research

> Nothing. The advance of science or technology cannot legitimate "class" and call it "order" so that a minority who holds power may use and squander the fruits of the earth while the vast majority are hard pressed even to survive and often justify their own misery as the will of God. I refuse to add my voice to that of the "peacemakers" who call upon the wretched of the earth to be resigned to their fate. (Freire, 1998, p. 93)

Answering the following question is foundational to ecopedagogical research: How can research guide education to center socioenvironmental justice and planetary sustainability and, thus, counter pedagogies without this foundation (Misiaszek, 2011, 2022) As Freire's quote above indicates, "sciences" and "technologies" that justify oppression and dominance should not be considered sciences, scientific, or beneficial tools (e.g., technologies). Freire discussed how banking educators teach absolute, unquestionable "rationality" of _S_ciences and _T_echnologies that, in turn, suppress humans' ingenuous curiosities that initiate research (Freire, 1998).

> As a manifestation present in the vital experience, human curiosity has been historically and socially constructed and reconstructed. Precisely because the advancement of innocence toward criticalness does not take place automatically, one of the primordial tasks of progressive educational practice is exactly the development of critical curiosity never satisfied or docile. That is the curiosity with which "we can defend ourselves from the "irrationality" resulting—from certain excesses of our highly technological

time's "rationality." This analysis, however, carries no falsely humanistic impetus against technology or science. On the contrary, it seeks to imbue technology with neither divine nor diabolic significance, but to look at it, or even observe it, in a critically curious manner. (Freire, 2004, p. 91)

Teaching to encourage and support ingenuous curiosities about how sciences and technologies should be reinvented, countered, and used, or not, is essential. Freire argued that reinventing sciences and technologies "presupposes an openness that allows for the revision of conclusions; it recognizes not only the possibility of making a new choice or a new evaluation but also the right to do so" (Freire, 1998).

We can take on endless scientific research and endeavors, but the fundamental question is which ones we *should* do. Problematizing the question of should is complex and contextual. Two grounding points of inquiry are (de)humanizing and (de)planetarizing aspects of research and associated endeavors. An obvious example is technologies that lead to weapons development which can be easily seen as dehumanizing and deplanetarizing. However, should jet-propelled research not happen because of its usage on fighter jets? Or because jet engines cause large amounts of pollution?

Problematizing what is taught as environmental "commonsense" but is false, or worse, outright fake, is through bottom-up dialogue and research that values ingenuous curiosity. Curiosities include asking why we have been taught this, but it is the opposite of what we are seeing.

To think correctly, in critical terms, is a requirement imposed by the rhythms of the gnostic circle on our curiosity, which, as it becomes more methodologically rigorous, progresses from ingenuity to what I have called "epistemological curiosity." Ingenuous curiosity, from which their results, without doubt, a certain kind of knowledge (even though not methodologically rigorous) is what characterizes "common sense" knowing. It is knowledge extracted from pure experience. To think correctly, from the teacher's point of view, implies respect for "common sense" knowing as it progresses from "common sense" to its higher stage. It also implies respect and stimulus for the creative capacity of the learner. (Freire, 1998, pp. 35–6)

Above, Freire is discussing commonsense from self-experiences as opposed to false commonsense discussed elsewhere in this book (e.g., neoliberal commonsense, commonsense of _D_evelopment, commonsense of coloniality). The former type of ingenuous commonsense is essential to disrupt the latter commonsense of oppressions and unsustainability. Disrupting unjust commonsense is very difficult due to various aspects, including its sheer complexities and ideological "no-alternative" strongholds discussed throughout this book. There is also "expert" manipulation and mystifying of sciences.

As she [the teacher] underscores fundamental importance of science, the progressive educator must also emphasize to poor boys and girls, as well as to the rich, the duty we all have to permanently question ourselves about in whose favor … or in favor of what, we make science. (Freire, 2004, p. 20)

An example of this emerged from my research in which people in Appalachia, United States, were being told by "experts" that water polluted by coal processing was healthy to drink and bath in, but people could see their friends and family having various health issues, including increased cancer rates in their communities (Misiaszek, 2011). Coal companies systematically made people question what they are seeing by mystifying sciences and making them feel stupid for not understanding and agreeing with knowledgeable "experts." Companies also portrayed the communities as ignorant and uneducated in the media and often criminalized their populations with phrases like, "well, there are a lot of criminals 'there.'" Research emerges from students' and teachers' curiosities about why something is happening, what is being said/taught, and why the answers to these two questions frequently conflict with one another. This research is done within ecopedagogical classrooms or individually through ecopedagogically literacy.

Freire (1998) reminds us that even though more methodological research is essential, all research begins with ingenuous curiosities.

I feel serious work, meticulous research, and critical reflection about dominant power, which is gaining increasing dimensions, have never been as needed as they are today. The activity of progressive intellectuals must never equate that of people who, recognizing the strength of obstacles, consider them to be insurmountable. That would be a fatalistic position, alien to the task of the progressive. Understanding obstacles as challenges, the progressive must search for appropriate answers. (Freire, 1997, p. 47)

Freire vehemently opposed neoliberal research, including pedagogical research leading to technocratic training, that is void of humanization or, I would add, planetarization.

Bottom-up research de-objectifies the oppressed to be seen as Subjects in their own "intervention in the world" with endless possible futures. Necessary environmental praxis can only emerge from bottom-up pedagogical research within ecopedagogical learning spaces, including while ecopedagogically reading. Ecopedagogues support students' critical curiosities to generate themes for meaningful, dialectic research within learning spaces.

Once again, there is no such thing as teaching without research and research without teaching. One inhabits the body of the other. As I teach, I continue to search and re-search. I submit myself to questioning. I research because I notice things, take cognizance of them. And in so doing, I intervene. And intervening, I educate and educate myself. I do research so as to know what I do not yet know and to communicate and proclaim what I discover. (Freire, 1998, p. 35)

Reinventing Freire's words above in ecopedagogical terms, bottom-up teaching *through* research is crucial, and research *through* teaching to deepen and widen first-person understandings of environmental violence for authentic praxis to emerge. This is expressed by Freire's play on the wording of "continu[ing] to search and re-search" for better praxis.

Unfortunately, increasingly prominent education for Development systematically discourages ecopedagogical research because it weakens ideological strongholds of neoliberalism and associated hegemony. Neoliberal methodologies grounded only on Sciences have been falsely equated as the only "legitimate" and "rigorous" scientific methodologies. The most harmful environmental pedagogical research are the ones politically guided by neoliberalist goals that dictate methodologies and predetermine what the results will be by bending the research for their desired outcomes. Such politics influence research to align education for Development are tools for teaching continuing socioenvironmental oppressions and planetary unsustainability. Neoliberalism is not the by-product of research for Development, but neoliberal-based research of education is essential to legitimize Development and vice versa. For Development to succeed, neoliberal research must delegitimize all other types, goals, and methodologies of research on (environmental) education. Research that leads to education for development becomes its enemy and, thus, is very much needed for environmental justice and sustainability.

Reading Media

Teaching ecopedagogical literacy includes reading environmental (mis)education outside formal and non-formal spaces, including media as public pedagogies (part of informal education). For example, how does the internet provide education for interpreting "realities?" This leads to questioning what are the politics touting certain "realities" and not others.

How are acts of environmental violence, social injustices, and connections between them portrayed or ignored on the internet, or worse, falsely portraying that socioenvironmental connections do not exist? How do websites cater (anti-) environmental information in diverse ways to varying audiences (i.e., users)? What websites do search engines (e.g., Google, Bing) give on the topic of environmental violence for the first ten or twenty results compared to the 100,000 to 100,010th results that almost no one will see? From such hierarchical results given to online users, what control and associated local-to-global power does Google have in a person's search for information? What information and websites are given to keep people scrolling downward on social media such as Facebook? What control does Facebook have within global Southern populations where they subsidize people's internet usage through their platform? This essentially has people equating the internet as Facebook. Problematizing the politics of dominant media is essential, as well as a better understanding of how media, including the internet, can be powerful educational tools for ecopedagogical praxis (Kahn & Kellner, 2006; Kahn, 2010).

Reading the media through critical lenses (e.g., critical media culture (see Fuchs, 2009; Kellner & Share, 2007), post-digitalism (Jandrić & Ford, 2022; Misiaszek et al., 2022, see Jandrić & Ford, 2020) helps to unveil falsities portrayed as "truths" about the existence, causes, and effects of unsustainable environmental violence. Critical/ecopedagogical literacy is increasingly important in today's intensifying global knowledge economies and post-truthism. Freire's notions of reading the word to read the world are currently as, or more, important within "virtual" spaces as compared to in-person ones. This includes, but is hardly limited to, social media content and algorithms for search engines' results and social media's matching users with postings (e.g., advertisements, (post-truth) information) and people to keep users scrolling downward.

CHAPTER SIX

Environmental Citizenships

Education as the practice of freedom—as opposed to education as the practice of domination—denies that man is abstract, isolated, independent and unattached to the world; it also denies that the world exists as a reality apart from people. (Freire, 2000, p. 81)

Ecopedagogy is an essential element of citizenship education and vice versa, as well as how actions for "development" are determined (Misiaszek, 2015, 2018). As previously discussed, public education largely emerged for teaching citizenship with often the unfortunate emphasis on teaching who are the "non-citizens," including not "full" citizens, and teaching for development. Teaching for _Development frequently justifies de-development for non-citizens without planetary sustainability. Ecopedagogies are essential for genuine freedom, participatory citizenship_ (locally-to-globally-to-planetary citizenship), and participatory democracy (Misiaszek, 2015, 2018; Gadotti & Torres, 2009). Teaching to both widen and localize (or deepen) who/what we consider "fellow citizens" help increase and strengthen our connections with one another as humans and with the rest of Nature.

Thinned democratic citizenry aligns with what Martin Carnoy (1997) argues below as incomplete democracy and, in turn, incomplete citizenship within neoliberal ideologies.

The "incomplete" democratic politics of neoliberalism- a politics reduced to enhancing isolated individuals' solitary competitiveness in a Darwinian struggle. Freire's state is *constructive,* one where citizens are reintegrated through forming new political and social networks based both on information *and* critical analysis of their own situation in the global environment. Freire's state is also one of *solidarity*, including the marginalized, even when the global market has no room for them and exclusionary local ideologies segregate them. (Carnoy, 1997, p. 11, emphasis in original)

Carnoy's arguments, partially through Freirean scholarship, focuses on State citizenship. However, his arguments are relevant within and between local-to-global citizenships that are thinned and "incomplete," along with participatory democracy, due to neoliberal globalization. Ecopedagogical problematizing of citizenships' democratic in/exclusion is, in part, deconstructing the sociohistories of oppressions and dominance of Nature and its thickening/thinning from globalizations. As Carnoy expresses, neoliberalism's impact is essential to unpack. This unpacking is foundational to ecopedagogies.

Freire below discusses the need for citizenship education to be taught dialectically for authentic praxis to emerge. Such teaching is through theoretical lenses, but the theories used must relate to students' meanings and realities or the lenses will be useless in teaching.

Fundamental background necessary for the full participation of any citizen in the development of the new society will be included in Basic Instruction. We are not talking about instruction in a school that simply prepares the learners for another school, but about a real education where the content is in a constant dialectical relation with the needs of the country. In this kind of education, knowledge, resulting in practical action, itself grows out of the unity between theory and practice. For this reason, it is not possible to divorce the process of learning from its own source within the lives of the learners themselves. (Freire, 1978, p. 42)

In other words, theories emerge from realities rather than detached scholarly work that is unrelatable and useable to better the world *within* planetary sustainability (Misiaszek, 2021). Rich contextuality is essential in ecopedagogical teaching, reading, and methodologies, including praxis for more-inclusive citizenships.

Citizenships

Similar to the contested terrains of globalizations, global citizenship and its education (GC/E) form contested terrains coinciding and conflicting with ecopedagogical tenets (Misiaszek, 2015, 2016, 2018). Beyond and including traditional national citizenship, more holistic citizenship education must focus on local-to-global socioenvironmental justice *with* local-to-planetary sustainability. This latter part is not tangentially added but must be saturated within citizenships education. Neither justice nor sustainability will be achieved with citizenship ideologies disregarding others as non-citizens. Citizenship ideologies of exclusion of distancing of "non-citizens" geographically, culturally, epistemologically, and linguistically, among other ways. The rest of Nature is included in these distancing ideologies. The question for ecopedagogues is how can "citizenship" be taught for not only opposing these ideologies but also reinventing "citizenship" for meaningful global-to-planetary inclusion without exception?

Throughout this book, I have discussed the need for citizenship education for ecopedagogy. Figure 1 ecopedagogy illustrates the intersectionality within and between local-to-planetary citizenship spheres for ecopedagogical work.

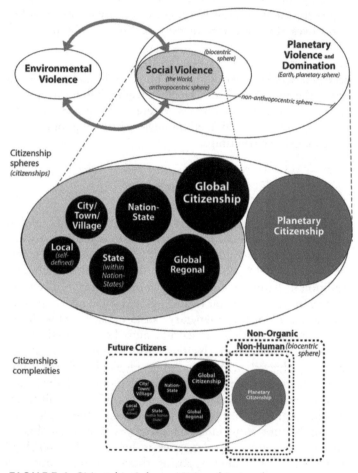

FIGURE 1 Citizenship Spheres (Citizenships) and Intersectionalities.

Planetary citizenship forms solidarity with the rest of Earth, as Earth holistically is considered a citizen (Gutiérrez & Prado, 1989; Gadotti, 2008b; Misiaszek, 2018, 2020) to achieve goals of sustainable development. There are numerous ways to understand planetary citizenship. Gadotti defined planetary citizenship as "an expression that was adopted to express a group of principles, values, attitudes and habits that reveal a new perception of Earth as a single community" (2008a, 2008b, 2008c). In his office at the Paulo Freire Institute, São Paulo around 2010, Gadotti initiated a discussion with me on planetary citizenship by arguing that if Earth is a citizen, it is the most oppressed, voiceless citizen. There are several unique aspects to planetary citizenship as compared to other citizenships. As I have explained, the rest of Nature/Earth does not "act" from sociohistorical reflexivity. Due to this, humans have planetary citizenship responsibilities for their actions done to Earth holistically that are not reciprocal *from* the rest of Nature.

Within citizenships, it is vital to have solidarity with one another as we are all connected with Earth holistically. Such planetary connectivity includes unpacking the complexities of respecting each other's vast diversity, including diverse citizenship framings, as well as the commonalities. When I speak of global and planetary citizenships, I am not devaluing the contextuality of other citizenship spheres, including traditional citizenship. This valuing aligns with Torres's (2017b) arguments that global citizenship needs to add value to national citizenship to be successful. It is the interconnectivity, especially with intensifying globalizations, that each other's actions, no matter the distances or differences, affect each other and Earth overall. For effective ecopedagogical praxis, we must collectively work together globally and planetarily. Ideologies and theories of citizenships help us do this inside and outside education. For example, to counter "development" within problematic citizenship framings that is for "us" on the backs of "them," some global citizenship models and all planetary citizenship models widen the "us" to all humans in the former and all of Earth in the latter.

Contested Terrain of GC/E

Utilizing other scholars' GCE work (Torres, 2017b; Shultz, 2007; Tarozzi & Torres, 2016), the term *critical* GC/E indicates the global and planetary connectedness for socioenvironmental justice and sustainability associated with praxis for social justice, environmental sustainability, and, specifically in this book's contexts, ecopedagogical goals. Critical GC educators teach students to have authentic roles of citizenships from their local communities to the world-Earth holistically. Returning to thickness/thinness terminology, thickening and widening students' citizenships is the goal of critical GCE. This thickening and widening is increasingly difficult with intensifying neoliberal globalization.

Countering neoliberal global citizenship is a crucial concern for critical GCE. Neoliberalism continues by diminishing protest against its oppressive processes. Vanishing protest is aided by banking education in the various ways discussed throughout this book. Othering people who suffer socioenvironmentally includes labeling them as "non-citizens," which, in turn, extinguishes possibilities of solidarity. A singular neoliberal future must also be ideologically entrenched through banking approaches. Postma (2006) argued that neoliberal caring for only one's own private sphere—thus, absent of any solidary for the oppressed, dominated othered. Without further explanation, caring for the rest of Nature is nil within neoliberalism (GC/E) (Postma, 2006). In various ways, the rest of Nature could be viewed as the slave(s) as characterized by Hegel. However, without the ability of neither reflectivity nor praxis, the non-anthroposphere cannot counter their masters' (i.e., humans, the world's) domination, in which slaves are "hosts" for parasitic masters' unjust power (Earth in this sentence). This leads to the question, "who" counters our unsustainable violence which has the rest of Nature as hosts of *D*evelopment? How do we ensure not to be/come parasite with the host being the rest of Nature?

Freire (1998) argued that education must have a "universal human ethic" which allows for commonalities for understanding, respecting, and (armed) love for one another,[1] as well as faith in humans (Darder, 2002).

> When I speak of a universal human ethic, however, I am speaking of something absolutely indispensable for human living and human social intercourse. In making this statement, I am aware of the critical voices of those who, because they do not know where I am coming from, consider me ingenuous and idealistic. In truth, I speak of a universal human ethic in the same way I speak of humanity's ontological vocation, which calls us out of and beyond ourselves. Or as I speak of our being as something constructed socially and historically and not there simply a priori. (Freire, 1998, p. 25)

Freire (1998) wrote later in the same book that what is also needed in education is to counter perverted dehumanizing neoliberal "ethics." This would include neoliberal GCE.

> The place upon which a new rebellion should be built is not the ethics of the marketplace with its crass insensitivity to the voice of genuine humanity but the ethics of universal human aspiration. The ethics of human solidarity. (Freire, 1998, p. 116)

Ecopedagogical reinventing Freire's terms here would widen the "ethics of human solidarity," also implying planetary solidarity.

Freire's (1998) "human ethic," in essence, is the grounding of critical GC/E by "speak[ing] of humanity's ontological vocation, which calls us out of and beyond ourselves." Torres (2017b, 2017a), in part, reinvented this universal human ethic in his arguments that for critical GC to be successful, there must be global commons that all humans share. Torres' (2017b) three *global commons* are given below.

1. Our planet is our only home, and we have to protect it through a global citizenship sustainable development education, moving from diagnosis and denunciation into action and policy implementation

2. global peace is an intangible cultural good of humanity with immaterial value. Global peace is a treasure of humanity

3. need to find ways that people who are all equal manage to live together democratically in a world growing evermore diverse, seeking to fulfill their individual and cultural interests and achieving their inalienable rights to life, liberty and the pursuit of happiness. (Torres, 2017b, p. 94)

With necessary reflexivity, we understand, respect, and care that everyone seeks to achieve these global commons in critical GCE. Tierney (2018) argues the need to teach global meaning-making with our "shared interest in sustainability" as a human instinct, which coincides with Torres's (2017a, 2017b) global common of needing to live within local environmentally healthy ecosystems.

Ecopedagogy is needed *within* critical GCE to teach toward achieving these global commons worldwide without exception and planetary sustainability beyond non-anthropocentric lenses. How can environmental pedagogues teach students to read globalizations distancing of socioenvironmental effects that "they" (e.g., the othered, the non-citizens) suffer from "our" actions? Although linguistically problematic, the "they" also includes the rest of Nature. A utopic ecopedagogical goal is that terms such as "they" (including also, "them," "their," and it('s)) to separate caring for socioenvironmental justice and unsustainability ultimately vanishes.

CHAPTER SEVEN

Final Words of Warning

I end this book with the spirit of Freire's arguments of unfinishedness. Ecopedagogies must be endlessly reinvented within Freire's essence, even when some reinventions counter the specifics of his work. This book is also unfinished. Without teaching to radically disrupt untethered environmental violence from the hegemonic upon the powerless, including the rest of Nature, socioenvironmental injustices, domination, and unsustainability will only intensify. True finishedness of the world will only occur if our actions toward environmental tipping points are not actively disrupted. This is because the world will no longer exist.

I have not provided specific projects as examples of ecopedagogical work. Instead, I focused on the characteristics of ecopedagogy through a diverse range of acts of unstainable environmental violence I have exemplified. I hope reading this book will help readers identify ecopedagogical approaches to environmental teaching and teaching which is not. As discussed throughout this book, identification is far from simple, as ecopedagogical work is not often labeled as such, and the label of being "critical" and/or "ecopedagogical" does not mean it truly is. Once shallow environmental pedagogies are identified, next will be the difficult but necessary task of ecopedagogically reinventing through the topics I have discussed in this book and beyond. I am referring to contextual reinventing of teaching through Freirean, ecopedagogical groundings when I use the term "beyond" here. As discussed initially in the introduction, this includes scholarship that coincides and conflicts with my arguments I have given in this book. It is without a doubt that Freire's work and the ecopedagogical field are growing in various ways despite forces, such as intensifying global neoliberalism, that impede this crucial work to help save Earth. My hope is that this book will help contribute toward this exceptionally vital planetary-wide goal. Similarly, as the editor with Carlos Alberto Torres of the Bloomsbury's *Freire in Focus* book series, my aim is that this series will do the same.

NOTES

Series Editors' Foreword

1 Paulo Freire, *Pedagogy of Indignation*. Boulder, CO: Paradigm Publishers, p. 25.

2 Gadotti, Moacir and Carlos AlbertoTorres, "Paulo Freire: Education for Development," *Development and Change*, 40 (6) (2009): pp. 1255–67.

Introduction

1 This includes the beginning of my 2020 Bloomsbury book *Ecopedagogy: Critical Environmental Teaching for Planetary Justice and Global Sustainable Development.*

Chapter 1

1 "Stars" can be viewed as referring to the larger universe, including Earth.

2 Although I problematize Illich's writing as gendered (i.e., "primitive/modern man"), there is the argument that maybe, to some degree, it is appropriately gendered due to socioenvironmental oppressions due to patriarchy. Orally I have argued that the gendered primitive and modern "Man" might not be negative as gendered because historically, it has been men who have furthered oppressions, injustices, and unsustainability compared to their female and other genders counterparts. However, it is probably best if this was contextual, and the

all-inclusive gendered masculine wording should be widened to "primitive/modern humans." For simplicity of reading, I will mostly use Illich's original wording for the rest of this book.

Chapter 6

1 Freire's "armed love" is described by Antonia Darder (2002) as the following, "that could be lively, forceful, and inspiring, while at the same time, critical, challenging, and insistent … [standing] in direct opposition to the insipid "generosity" of teachers or administrators who would blindly adhere to a system of schooling that fundamentally transgresses every principle of cultural and economic democracy" (p. 3).

REFERENCES

Antunes, Â. B., Pini, F., Padilha, P. R., & Couto, S. 2019. Fertilizing the unusual (The praxis of a connective organization). In C. A. Torres (ed.), *Wiley Handbook of Paulo Freire*. New Jersey: Wiley-Blackwell, 565–83.

Apple, M. W., & Au, W. 2009. Politics, theory, and reality in critical pedagogy. In R. Cowen & A. M. Kazamias (eds.), *International Handbook of Comparative Education*. Dordrecht: Springer Science + Media Studies, 991–1007.

Apple, M. W. 1999. Between neoliberalism and neoconservatism: Education and conservatism in a global context. In N. C. Burbules & C. A. Torres (eds.), *Globalization and Education: Critical Perspectives*. New York: Routledge, 57–78.

Apple, M. W. 2000. *Official Knowledge: Democratic Education in a Conservative Age*, New York: Routledge.

Apple, M. W. 2004. *Ideology and Curriculum*, New York: Routledge.

Apple, M. W. 2006. *Educating the "Right" Way: Markets, Standards, God, and Inequality*, New York: Routledge.

Aronowitz, S. 1998. Introduction: Pedagogy of freedom: Ethics, democracy, and civic courage. In P. Freire (ed.), Lanham, MD: Rowman & Littlefield, 1–19.

Assié-Lumumba, N. D. T. 2017. The Ubuntu paradigm and comparative and international education: epistemological challenges and opportunities in our field. *Comparative Education Review*, 61, 1–21.

Au, W. W., & Apple, M. W. 2007. Reviewing policy: Freire, critical education, and the environmental crisis. *Educational Policy*, 21, 457–70.

Bohorquez, I. 2008. Untested feasibility in Paulo Freire: Behind the profile of a dream. In C. A. Torres & P. Noguera (eds.), *Social Justice Education for Teachers: Paulo Freire and the Possible Dream*. Rotterdam: Sense Publishers, 177–90.

Carnoy, M. 1997. Foreword. In P. Freire & A. M. A. Freire (eds.), *Pedagogy of the Heart*. New York: Continuum, 7–19.

Clark, B., & Foster, J. B. 2010. Marx's ecology in the 21st century. *World Review of Politial Economy*, 1, 142–56.

Connell, R. 2007. *Southern Theory: The Global Dynamics of Knowledge in Social Science*, Cambridge: Polity.

Connell, R. 2013. Using southern theory: Decolonizing social thought in theory, research and application. *Planning Theory*, 13, 210–23.

Connell, R. 2014. Epistemologies of the South: Justice against epistemicide by Boaventura de Sousa Santos. *American Journal of Sociology*, 120, 949–51.

Darder, A. 2002. *Reinventing Paulo Feire: A Pedagogy of Love*, Boulder, CO: Westview Press.

Delgado, R. 1989. Storytelling for oppositionists and others: A plea for narrative. *Michigan Law Review*, 87, 2411–41.

Derni, A. 2008. The ecolinguistic paradigm: An integrationist trend in language study. *International Journal of Language Society and Culture*, (24), 21–30.

Epstein-Halevi, D. Y., Misiaszek, G. W., Kelly, H., Shah, S., Mugarura, C., & Walsh, L. 2018. Building eco-social resilience in the face of climate change and drought: How permaculture pedagogy and praxis can benefit rural communities and their environment. In W. Leal Filho (ed.), *Climate Change Management*. London: Springer.

Fanon, F. 1963. *The Wretched of the Earth*, New York: Grove Press.

Fanon, F. 1967. *Black Skin, White Masks*, New York: Grove Press.

Figueroa, R., & Harding, S. G. 2003. *Science and Other Cultures: Issues in Philosophies of Science and Technology*, New York: Routledge.

Fill, A., & Mühlhäusler, P. 2001. *The Ecolinguistics Reader: Language, Ecology, and Environment*, London: Continuum.

Fill, A. 2001. Language and ecology: Ecolinguistic perspectives for 2000 and beyond. In D. Graddol (ed.), *Applied Linguistics for the 21st Century*. Open University, School of Education, AILA Review, 60–75.

Freire, P., & Freire, A. M. A. 1997. *Pedagogy of the Heart*, New York: Continuum.

Freire, P. 1978. *Pedagogy in Process: The Letters to Guinea-Bissau*, New York: Seabury Press.

Freire, P. 1985. *The Politics of Education: Culture, Power, and Liberation*, South Hadley, MA: Bergin & Garvey.

Freire, P. 1992. *Pedagogy of Hope*, New York: Continuum.

Freire, P. 1993. *Pedagogy of the City*, New York: Continuum.

Freire, P. 1996. *Letters to Cristina: Reflections on My Life and Work*, New York: Routledge.

Freire, P. 1997. *Pedagogy of the Heart*, New York: Continuum.

Freire, P. 1998. *Pedagogy of Freedom: Ethics, Democracy, and Civic Courage*, Lanham, MD: Rowman & Littlefield.

Freire, P. 1998a. *Pedagogy of Freedom: Ethics, Democracy, and Civic Courage*, Lanham, MD: Rowman & Littlefield.

Freire, P. 1998b. *Politics and Education*, Los Angeles: UCLA Latin American Center Publications.

Freire, P. 1998c. *Teachers as Cultural Workers: Letters to Those Who Dare Teach*, Boulder, CO: Westview Press.

Freire, P. 2000. *Pedagogy of the Oppressed*, New York: Continuum.

Freire, P. 2004. *Pedagogy of Indignation*, Boulder, CO: Paradigm Publishers.

Freitas, A. L. S. D. 2012. Conscientization [Conscientização]. In D. R. Streck, E. Redin, & J. J. Zitkoski (eds.), *Paulo Freire Encyclopedia*, Lanham, MD: Rowman & Littlefield, 69–71.

Fuchs, C. 2009. Information and communication technologies and society: A contribution to the critique of the political economy of the internet. *European Journal of Communication, 24*, 69–87.

Gadotti, M., & Torres, C. A. 2009. Paulo Freire: Education for development. *Development and Change, 40*, 1255–67.

Gadotti, M. 1996. *Pedagogy of Praxis: A Dialectical Philosophy of Education*, Albany: SUNY Press.

Gadotti, M. 2008a. *Education for Sustainability: A Critical Contribution to the Decade of Education for Sustainable Development*. São Paulo, Brazil: University of São Paulo, Paulo Freire Institute.

Gadotti, M. 2008b. *Education for Sustainable Development: What We Need to Learn to Save the Planet*, São Paulo, Brazil: Instituto Paulo Freire.

Gadotti, M. 2008c. What we need to learn to save the planet. *Journal of Education for Sustainable Development, 2*, 21–30.

Giroux, H. A. 2001. *Theory and Resistance in Education: Towards a Pedagogy for the Opposition*, Westport, CT: Bergin & Garvey.

Goodman, R. T., & Saltman, K. J. 2002. *Strange Love: Or How We Learn to Stop Worrying and Love the Market*, Lanham, MD: Rowman & Littlefield.

Gutiérrez, F., & Prado, C. 1989. *Ecopedagogia e cidadania planetária. (Ecopedagogy and Planetarian Citizenship)*, São Paulo, Cortez.

Harding, S. G. 1991. *Whose Science? Whose Knowledge?: Thinking from Women's Lives*, Ithaca, NY: Cornell University Press.

Harding, S. G. 1998. *Is Science Multicultural?: Postcolonialisms, Feminisms, and Epistemologies*, Bloomington: Indiana University Press.

Harding, S. G. 2006. *Science and Social Inequality: Feminist and Postcolonial Issues*, Urbana: University of Illinois Press.

Horton, M., Freire, P., Bell, B., Gaventa, J., & Peters, J. M. 1990a. *We Make the Road by Walking: Conversations on Education and Social Change*, Philadelphia: Temple University Press.

Horton, M., Kohl, J., & Kohl, H. R. 1990b. *The Long Haul: An Autobiography*, New York: Doubleday.

Illich, I. 1983. *Deschooling Society*, New York: Harper Colophon.

International Organization for Migration (IOM). 2014. *IOM Outlook on Migration, Environment and Climate Change.* Geneva: International Organization for Migration.

Jandrić, P., & Ford, D. R. 2020. Postdigital ecopedagogies: Genealogies, contradictions, and possible futures. *Postdigital Science and Education*, 4, 692–710.

Jandrić, P., & Ford, D. R. 2022. *Postdigital Ecopedagogies*, London: Springer.

Jickling, B., & Wals, A. E. J. 2008. Globalization and environmental education: Looking beyond sustainable development. *Journal of Curriculum Studies*, 40, 1–21.

Kahn, R., and Kellner, D. M. 2006. Opositional politics and the internet: A critical/reconstructive approach. In M. G. Durham & D. Kellner (eds.), *Media and Cultural Studies: Keyworks*. Rev. ed. Malden, MA: Blackwell, 703–25.

Kahn, R. 2010. *Critical Pedagogy, Ecoliteracy, and Planetary Crisis: The Ecopedagogy Movement*, New York: Peter Lang.

Kellner, D., & Share, J. 2007. Critical media literacy is not an option. *Learning Inquiry*, 1, 59–69.

Macedo, D. 2005. Introduction to the Anniversary Edition. In P. Freire (ed.), *Pedagogy of the Oppressed*. New York: Continuum, 11–28.

Mayo, P. 1999. *Gramsci, Freire and Adult Education: Possibilities for Transformative Action*, New York: Zed Books.

McLaren, P. 2007a. Conservation, class struggle, or both: A response to C.A. Bowers. *Capitalism, Nature, and Socialism*, 18, 99–108.

McLaren, P. 2007b. Peter McLaren responds. *Capitalism, Nature, and Socialism*, 18, 119–20.

Memmi, A. 1991. *The Colonizer and the Colonized*, Boston: Beacon Press.

Misiaszek, G. W. 2011. *Ecopedagogy in the Age of Globalization: Educators' Perspectives of Environmental Education Programs in the Americas which Incorporate Social Justice Models*. PhD Dissertation, University of California, Los Angeles: University of California.

Misiaszek, G. W. 2012. Transformative environmental education within social justice models: Lessons from comparing adult ecopedagogy within North and South America. In D. N. Aspin, J. Chapman, K. Evans, & R. Bagnall (eds.), *Second International Handbook of Lifelong Learning*. London: Springer, 423–40.

Misiaszek, G. W. 2015. Ecopedagogy and citizenship in the age of globalisation: Connections between environmental and global citizenship education to save the planet. *European Journal of Education*, 50, 280–92.

Misiaszek, G. W. 2016. Ecopedagogy as an element of citizenship education: The dialectic of global/local spheres of citizenship and critical environmental pedagogies. *International Review of Education*, 62, 587–607.

Misiaszek, G. W. 2018. *Educating the Global Environmental Citizen: Understanding Ecopedagogy in Local and Global Contexts*, New York: Routledge.

Misiaszek, G. W. 2020a. Countering post-truths through ecopedagogical literacies: Teaching to critically read "development" and "sustainable development." *Educational Philosophy and Theory*, 52, 747–58.

MIsiaszek, G. W. 2020b. *Ecopedagogy: Critical Environmental Teaching for Planetary Justice and Global Sustainable Development*, London: Bloomsbury.

Misiaszek, G. W. 2020c. Ecopedagogy: Teaching critical literacies of "development," "sustainability," and "sustainable development." *Teaching in Higher Education,* 25, 615–32.

Misiaszek, G. W. 2020d. Locating and diversifying modernity: Deconstructing knowledges to counter Development for a few. In M. A. Peters, T. Besley, P. Jandrić, & X. Zhu (eds.), *Knowledge Socialism: The Rise of Peer Production: Collegiality, Collaboration, and Collective Intelligence.* Singapore: Springer Nature, 253–76.

Misiaszek, G. W. 2022. An ecopedagogical, ecolinguistical reading of the Sustainable Development Goals (SDGs): What we have learned from Paulo Freire. *Educational Philosophy and Theory,* 54(13), 2297–2311.

Misiaszek, G. W. 2022. Contested terrains of environmental pedagogies: Comparing ecopedagogy, education for sustainable development (ESD) and environmental education. In L. I. Misiaszek, R. F. Arnove, & C. A. Torres (eds.), *Emergent Trends in Comparative Education: The Dialectic of the Global and the Local.* Lanham, MD: Rowman & Littlefield, 23–39.

Misiaszek, G. W., Epstein-Halevi, D. Y., Reindl, S., & Jolly, T. L. 2022. Ecopedagogy disrupting postdigital divides of (neo) Coloniality, (eco)Racism, and anthropocentricism: A case study In P. Jandrić & D. R. Ford (eds.), *Postdigital Ecopedagogies.* London: Springer, 121–45.

Misiaszek, G. W., & Torres, C. A. 2012. Ideology [Ideologia]. In D. R. Streck, E. Redin, & J. J. Zitkoski (eds.), *Paulo Freire Encyclopedia.* Lanham, MD: Rowman & Littlefield, 185–6.

Misiaszek, G. W., & Torres, C. A. 2019. Ecopedagogy: The missing chapter of pedagogy of the oppressed. In C. A. Torres (ed.), *Wiley Handbook of Paulo Freire.* New Jersey: Wiley-Blackwell, 463–88.

Moore, J. W. 2017. The Capitalocene, Part I: On the nature and origins of our ecological crisis. *Journal of Peasant Studies,* 44, 594–630.

Morrow, R. A., & Torres, C. A. 2002. *Reading Freire and Habermas,* New York: NY, Teachers College Press.

Morrow, R. A. 2019. Paulo Freire and the "logic of reinvention": Power, the state, and education in the global age. In C. A. Torres (ed.), *Wiley handbook of Paulo Freire.* New Jersey: Wiley-Blackwell, 445–62.

Osowski, C. I. 2012. Limit-situations [Situaçôes-Limites]. In D. R. Streck, E. Redin, & J. J. Zitkoski (eds.), *Paulo Freire Encyclopedia*. Lanham, MD: Rowman & Littlefield, 216–17.

Passos, L. A. 2012. Generating theme [Tema Gerdor]. In D. R. Streck, E. Redin, & J. J. Zitkoski (eds.), *Paulo Freire Encyclopedia*. Lanham: Rowman & Littlefield, 158–60.

Peters, M. A. 2017. Education in a post-truth world. *Educational Philosophy and Theory*, 49, 563–6.

Peters, M. A., Rider, S., Hyvönen, M., & Besley, T. 2018. *Post-Truth, Fake News: Viral Modernity & Higher Education*, Singapore: Springer.

Postma, D. W. 2006. *Why Care for Nature?: In Search of an Ethical Framework for Environmental Responsibility and Education*, New York: Springer.

Rhoads, R. A., & Torres, C. A. 2006. *The University, State, and Market the Political Economy of Globalization in the Americas*, Stanford, CA: Stanford University Press.

Rosa, H. 2003. Social acceleration: Ethical and political consequences of a desynchronized high-speed society. *Constellations*, 10, 3–33.

Said, E. W. 1979. *Orientalism*, New York: Vintage Books.

Santos, B. D. S. 2012. Public sphere and epistemologies of the South. *Africa Development*, 37, 43–67.

Santos, B. D. S. 2014. *Epistemologies of the South: Justice against Epistemicide*, Boulder, CO: Paradigm Publishers.

Santos, B. D. S. 2016. Epistemologies of the South and the future. *From the European South: A Transdisciplinary Journal of Postcolonial Humanities*, 17–29.

Santos, B. D. S. 2018. *The End of the Cognitive Empire: The Coming of Age of Epistemologies of the South*, Durham, NC: Duke University Press.

Saul, J. R. 1995. *The Unconscious Civilization*, Concord: House of Anansi Press.

Scherr, A. 2005. Social subjectivity and mutual recognition as basic terms of a critical theory of education. In G. Fischman, P. McLaren, H. Sunker, & C. Lankshear (eds.), *Critical Theories, Radical Pedagogies, and Global Conflicts*. Lanham, MD: Rowman & Littlefield.

Schugurensky, D. 2011. *Paulo Freire*, London: Bloomsbury.

Shultz, L. 2007. Educating for global citizenship: Conflicting agendas and understandings. *Alberta Journal of Educational Research,* 53, 248–58.

Singh, N. M. 2019. Environmental justice, degrowth and post-capitalist futures. *Ecological Economics,* 163, 138–42.

Smith, G. H. 2000. Protecting and respecting Indigenous knowledge. In M. Battiste (ed.), *Reclaiming Indigenous Voice and Vision.* Vancouver: University of British Columbia Press, 209–44.

Solorzano, D. G., & Yosso, T. J. 2002. A critical race counterstory of race, racism, and affirmative action. *Equity & Excellence in Education,* 35, 155–68.

Stibbe, A. 2012. Ecolinguistics and globalization. In N. Coupland (ed.), *The Handbook of Language and Globalization.* West Sussex: Wiley-Blackwell, 413–18.

Stibbe, A. 2014. An ecolinguistic approach to critical discourse studies. *Critical Discourse Studies,* 11, 117–28.

Stromquist, N. P. 2002. *Education in a Globalized World: The Connectivity of Economic Power, Technology, and Knowledge,* Lanham, MD: Rowman & Littlefield.

Tarozzi, M., & Torres, C. A. 2016. *Global Citizenship Education and the Crises of Multiculturalism: Comparative Perspectives,* London: Bloomsbury Academic.

Teodoro, A., & Torres, C. A. 2007. Introduction: Critique and utopia in the sociology of education. In C. A.Torres & A. Teodoro (eds.), *Critique and Utopia: New Developments in the Sociology of Education in the Twenty-first Century.* Lanham, MD: Rowman & Littlefield, 1–10.

Tierney, R. J. 2018. Toward a Model of Global Meaning Making. *Journal of Literacy Research,* 50, 397–422.

Torres, C. A. 2009. *Globalizations and Education: Collected Essays on Class, Race, Gender, and the State,* New York: Teachers College Press.

Torres, C. A. 2011. Public universities and the neoliberal common sense: Seven iconoclastic theses. *International Studies in Sociology of Education,* 21, 177–97.

Torres, C. A. 2013. Emerging global citizenship education agenda. *Newsletter of the World Council of Comparative Education Societies (WCCES),* 2, 11–13.

Torres, C. A. 2014. *First Freire: Early Writings in Social Justice Education,* New York: Teachers College Press.

Torres, C. A. 2015. Oppressor and oppressed: Logical dialectical categories? Tribute to Paulo Freire. *Sinéctica* [Online], 45. Available: http://www.scielo.org.mx/scielo.php?script=sci_artt ext&pid=S1665-109X2015000200008&nrm=iso [accessed January 31, 2018].

Torres, C. A. 2017a. Education for global citizenship. *Oxford Research Encyclopedia of Education*. Oxford: Oxford University Press. Available: https://oxfordre.com/education/view/10.1093/ acrefore/9780190264093.001.0001/acrefore-9780190264 093-e-91 [accessed October 31, 2022].

Torres, C. A. 2017b. *Theoretical And Empirical Foundations of Critical Global Citizenship Education*, New York: Routledge.

Warren, K. J. 2000. *Ecofeminist Philosophy: A Western Perspective on What it is and Why it Matters*, Lanham, MD: Rowman & Littlefield.

White, H. V. 1973. *Metahistory: The Historical Imagination in Nineteenth-Century Europe*, Baltimore, MD: Johns Hopkins University Press.

Whiting, K., Konstantakos, L., Misiaszek, G. W., Simpson, E., & Carmona, L. 2018. Education for the sustainable global citizen: What can we learn from stoic philosophy and Freirean environmental pedagogies? *Education Sciences*, 8, 204.

INDEX